AGES OF SUFFOCATION:

Remembered dreams

(Based on a true life story)

UZO AMAKA

Acknowledgements

This book is dedicated to my siblings, thank you for all
your love and support. I love you.
To my two beautiful children, you are my rainbow, my
sunshine, my peace, my joy. Mommy loves you.
And lastly, Obim, thank you for being my rock!
Afulu gi nanya (Afurum gi nanya)

Child voice of Oma
(10 year period)

Teenage voice of Oma
(5 year period)

Adult voice of Oma
(10 Year period)

One

AGE 4 - 13

We entered the living room and Floressa, our stepmother, "The Giant" (as we saw her) was sitting on the couch waiting for us. Floressa was a beautiful woman; she was six feet, two inches and light-skinned, which equated to beauty and class in Nigeria. She had short, permed hair, kept long, manicured fingernails and long, pedicured toenails. It was her routine to paint her nails every Saturday, and do her cooking on Sundays, which we girls were required to assist her with so we could learn how to cook. Floressa prided herself on her fine cooking skills, her sophistication, and upper-class etiquette, so her expectations were that these same virtues would come naturally to us girls at all times. In her view, we, as her step-kids, were a reflection of her.

"Where did you guys get those biscuits?" Floressa asked in a mellow but stern tone.

Fear gripped us as we stood there, speechless. She must have been standing on the balcony which was on the top floor of our four-story house. She must have seen us walking back, stopping at Grandma's and buying the biscuits. Floressa was the type of person who expected us to come up and show her the money that was given to us by our grandmother, before we bought the biscuits and we hadn't done that.

"Am I not asking you guys a question? I said, where did you get the biscuits you're eating?" Floressa shouted as she got up from the couch and headed towards us.

Ada summoned the courage to speak. "Grandma gave us 50 kobo and we bought biscuits with it." I could hear the fear trembling through her voice; Uche and I were frozen in place. We knew what awaited us next.

AGE 24 - 33

It's September 2005 in Mountain View, California on a sunny afternoon. I am in the middle of my second visit with my church counselor, June.

"My step-mother was never nice to me. In fact, I believe she hated my existence." *Oh my goodness! I had totally forgotten about that!* I think to myself. I had forgotten about the feelings I had about Mommy Floressa - the fear I lived with as a child.

"Oma, tell me what happened next." June says. I stare at her in disbelief. Why? Why has she made me open this dark wound that wasn't even the issue that brought me to see her? I just wanted to speak with a professional about why women generally seem to hate me at first sight.

June is in her early to mid-fifties, with light brown eyes, and shoulder-length, dark brown hair. She is a bit overweight, but she seems comfortable with it. She is about five-feet, five; at least it looks that way from where she sits. Wearing a black skirt suit, she's sitting across from me in a soft plush gray chair. She has a notepad and pen in hand, looking at me with intense curiosity, waiting for me to finish my story.

"I'm sorry, June, but I didn't want to talk about my upbringing. I actually just wanted to find out if there was anything I may be doing on my part to emit vibes of being 'stuck up' towards other women."

After all, June isn't a licensed psychologist or shrink. She was just listed in the church staffing roster as a counselor.

"Oma, you mentioned to me that you had observed your older sister Ada being beaten bloody by your step-mother. Tell me what happened leading up to that."

I can't hold my tears in any longer. I start to weep helplessly in my chair, falling to my knees, with my head collapsed in my hands. I remember! I suddenly remember everything. Moments I had forgotten, moments I hadn't forgotten but are clearer now; it was as if my brain has regurgitated a flow of bad memories all at once in a single moment. I never wanted these memories relived; I was doing just fine, nineteen years later. But now I remember thoughts that probably would have stayed hidden had I never come to see June.

"Oma, tell me about your childhood," June says as she hands me a box of tissues. "Tell me why you're crying, and please, take your time."

Oh boy! I think, *I don't even know where to begin.*

AGE 4 - 13

It was 1986, a bright, sunny Saturday morning in Lagos, Nigeria, and my older sisters Ada, Uche and I had just gotten our hair woven with thread. Our hair was so tightly woven, you could see the veins on our foreheads, but we were used to it, and as far as we were concerned, we looked perfect. Our clothes were clean, our hair was done, and we were joyfully walking back home from the hair salon. Nine-year-old Ada was in a dark blue, ankle-length, loose-fitting skirt and a short sleeved yellow top with sandals; Uche, who was eight, had on a blue below-knee length dress with white polka dots and red ribbon at the center neckline with brown closed-toe shoes. I was seven years old, and I wore my favorite red knickers and pink-flowered short sleeved shirt and my white tennis shoes.

We stopped over to see our grandmother whose house was right next to ours. She was sitting outside in her special chair, which only she was allowed to sit in, watching passers-by. Grandma enjoyed sitting and watching for the vendors selling food items on top of their heads, like bread, raw meat or ready-made meals such as softly cooked beans with a peppered sauce known as "Ago-in Beans" for breakfast. I enjoyed watching her call on some of the vendors at times to buy food items for her house, like starch used to iron clothes, or 'Ugu' leaves used to make a melon-seed soup. She was such a good haggler. She could make someone sell a piece of first-rate meat at half the price, and the seller would leave with a look of bewilderment on their face. It was great. My sisters and I walked up to her.

"Good morning, Grandma!" we chorused.

"Ndewo, my daughters, how are you doing? You look so beautiful today; look how nice your hair is. Did you just do it?" Grandma asked.

"Yes, Grandma!" Uche quickly said with a smile.

"Very nice…very nice! What about your mommy? How is she?" Grandma asked referring to Floressa.

"She's fine, Grandma. She's upstairs," Ada said.

"Ok, tell her I said well done, ok? She's doing well taking care of you guys."

"Yes, Ma!"

Grandma then reached into her bosom, pulled out some bills, unfolded them and handed us fifty kobo each. "Take, use this to buy some sweets or biscuits, ok?"

"Thank you, Grandma!" Ada, Uche and I joyfully shouted in harmony and dashed off towards a food stand next door selling cookies, candy, biscuits, canned milk and such. We each got packets of biscuits, opened them excitedly and enjoyed them as we made our way up the winding metal staircase of our house. We were most likely going to watch one of the many movies Dad had brought back home from America. Our favorites at the time were the Disney sing-a-long songs series.

Upon entering our house, we noticed Floressa sitting in the living room with a stern look on her face. We had become accustomed to frequent beatings from Floressa for any reason or mood she might have been in. She was likely to slap us across the face for not finding something she sent us to get and give us a good beating for not coming into the kitchen with her when she was cooking. But on this particular day the beatings took a turn.

"Am I not asking you guys a question? I said, where did you get the biscuits you're eating?" Floressa shouted as she got up from the couch and headed towards us.

Ada summoned the courage to speak. "Grandma gave us 50 kobo and we bought biscuits with it."

Instantly, Floressa slapped Ada across the face. Then she began to hit Uche over her head with a closed fist, forcing Uche onto the wall behind her. She then slapped me across my face, which felt like a thousand bee stings at once. She turned back to Ada and pushed her to the floor and began hitting her. I remember her coming back to me and beating me all over my back and face and then I blacked out, not remembering how we ended up in our bedroom.

The curtains were closed and the room was dark. Ada was in the corner between my bed and the closet, and Floressa was in front of her, slapping her continuously, yelling at her words that escaped me as her voice seemed muffled and distant. Uche and I watched helplessly as Ada took the brunt of the beating that day. Ada's hair had come loose and the undone threads covered her face, and she had bloody welts all over her from Floressa's fingernails scratching her as she was being slapped. I noticed Ada wasn't crying anymore, she had been beaten so badly that her eyes just had a glassy gaze and she stared blankly straight ahead in the direction of Floressa's stomach area; that's how tall she was.

"Foolish girls! Let me see you spend money next time without telling me first!" Floressa yelled, then stomped out of our room and slammed the bedroom door.

Ada fell to the floor against the wall and held her head between her knees and chest and cried helplessly. We stayed in our room silent the rest of the day. Dad was in America.

AGE 24 - 33

June sits behind her desk in silence, as I let out all my emotions. I stop crying and am mostly in a daze. I have never shared this story with anyone until now.

"What are you thinking right now?" June asks as softly as her voice allows.

"Thinking?" I ask, wondering if my thoughts even matter right now. I am more worried about what this slew of new emotions is doing to me physically. My heart is palpitating, my breathing is shallow, my hands are trembling, and I am feeling emotionally numb, not wanting to accept all that I have just dredged up. It seems some part of my brain got a trigger from something, a word, a feeling, a reaction...I can't quite be sure but I'm flabbergasted at my sudden recall of this memory.

"Yes, Oma, thinking, feeling? Tell me what's going on in your mind right now," June asks.

"I don't know, June, I really don't...I'm feeling everything...I know I'm scared right now."

"Scared?" June asks. "Why do you feel scared? "

"Well...I don't know if it's fear, or what, but I just feel unsettled. I think the fear is from the fact that I cannot control my thoughts and how I feel about them. I don't like it."

"Ok, Oma. Let's see if we can pick this up again next week," June says as she ends our session.

I hate this. How is it ok to stop mid-emotion to be 'picked up' next week? How very unnatural. "Sure, we'll see you next week, June. Thank you for your time."

I leave her office knowing I am not going to go back.

AGE 15 - 19

As an adolescent, transitioning from schooling in Nigeria to schooling in America was one of the toughest changes for me. I was twelve years old when I returned to the U.S and junior high school was very different than the one I was used to. Kids were so cruel; I was often mocked by my peers.

"You're so black, you sweat coffee...hahaha," a student once said to me as I was walking down the hall, and other kids laughed and pointed as I sped off to hide in a bathroom.

"Can I ask you a question? Did you ride lions to school in Africa?" another student asked during English class and the whole class laughed. Worse yet, the teacher didn't even scold him. That was very unusual to me, because it was practically impossible for students to talk while a teacher was teaching in Nigeria without getting into trouble, let alone mock a student.

"How does it feel to wear clothes?" another girl asked when I was standing in line at the cafeteria for lunch, while the other kids in line laughed.

I was so glad when junior high was over. It had been dreadful. I started to come into my own by high school;

there were mostly new kids. Only a few had transferred from the junior high I went to so very few students knew I was from Nigeria unless I told them, or except when I spoke and they could hear my accent. And even then, they'd ask reasonable questions like, "How long have you been here? Do you like America? What's Africa like?"

It was like a breath of fresh air to be with new students, a bit more mature. Of course, there were still the lingering 'bad eggs' here and there who would make fun of my accent or my hair, and as time went on, I started to notice that those 'bad eggs' were all girls.

"Girl, Remy doesn't like you because she heard her man talking about you with his boys, telling them that you were the finest girl in class," my then best friend Tamika would tell me, comforting me after a brief verbal encounter with another female. Tamika and I became friends on the first day of English class; she sat next to me, asked me my name, and then started talking to me as if we'd been friends for years. I liked that. Tamika always had my back; she fought my battles when other girls tried to mock me.

"Girl, you ain't shit," Tamika once confronted another girl during History class as the girl insinuated that I smelled. "Your fat ass is what smells, stupid ass bitch!" Tamika continued.

"Who the fuck was talking to your ass? All I said was something stinks. Why you feeling all insecure and shit?" the other girl shouted. Both girls went on and on, cursing each other out, to the entertainment of the whole class. Even the teacher had a hard time controlling them for a while. Hard to believe Tamika was a Jehovah's Witness the way she was cursing the other girl out. I had found a true friend in Tamika during high school, and her friendship helped me hold my head a bit higher as high school progressed.

By sophomore year, our friendship-duo had developed into a larger group. Michelle and Rachel (the twins) were the 'jocks' of the group; they played basketball and had the same striving I did to get into college. Victor, was the 'pretty-boy Mexican' in the group. He and I were pretty close, but never dated. Mayumi, the 'mediator', was always calming situations down between one person or another. Kiona was the 'Michael Jackson fanatic'; there was rarely a day that went by when she hadn't included Michael Jackson's name regardless of what we might have been discussing. I found that so endearing of her.

Saanay was the cute gullible one, with long beautiful hair and almost unaware of her beauty. Nakia was the 'mama's girl' but in a good way. Almost everything she did, she'd want to make sure her mom would be proud of her for it. Picking a class, dating a boy, what she wore. I admired how confident she felt about needing her mother's approval. Chris was the 'adorable white boy' of the group. He was soft-spoken, generous and was one of the first kids in our school to have an interracial relationship. He dated a black girl who wasn't in our group and they dated all through high school. He loved her so much; it was almost annoying how cute they were.

And then there was Kree. Now Kree was the 'risk taking, fun-loving, joke-telling, white boy-loving' girl in the group. There was no truth or dare game we played where she didn't take the most risks. We once dared her to streak during lunch-time and without so much as a hiccup, she did. Another instance, we all sat outside the commuter train station, we dared her to go up and kiss a perfect stranger, hoping she'd bow-out of the game to lose. Nope, she walked right up to a tall white man, maybe in his early twenties and just getting off a train. Kree said a few words to him, and five seconds later, they were kissing. All our mouths dropped open in shock. When she came back over to the group, I asked her how she did that and she wouldn't say. She just smiled in silence. Later, when the rest of the group had left and it was just Kree and me waiting for a bus, I asked her again what she said to him.

"Well, I told him my friends over there bet me $20 that I couldn't get a kiss from him and begged him not to let me lose the bet." She giggled as she told me. "So he kissed me and said, 'Hey, go get your $20.' Shit, I couldn't tell him I was doing that shit for free."

We both laughed. Her lack of fear astonished me and I admired it. They were all my friends and I knew I wouldn't have been so lucky to have them if it hadn't been for Tamika Jones. I had gone from having one friend in junior high, to having ten best friends. Now, by no stretch of the imagination were we the 'cool' kids in school, but I may venture to say that we were the closest and had the most fun.

During sophomore year at age sixteen, I had my first boyfriend, Jawa. I met him on a Saturday afternoon at a flea market where his parents were selling vegetarian food from a food truck. I hadn't met him before as he didn't attend my high school. He had a dark complexion, a soft, smooth voice, and he was gentle in every sense with me, as if I were delicate. He didn't rush our first kiss, which happened about a month into dating. He knew I was still a virgin and respected my pleas every time I'd ask him to stop if our kissing got too passionate - though I was more scared than I was innocent in desiring sex. After about a year and some months of dating, I lost my virginity to him. The sensation of having another human part inside of me was both scary and exhilarating and I felt like a new person after that.

Jawa and I dated for two and a half years. We grew apart by the time I got into university and his lack of desire to go to college turned me completely off.

In college I had my second long relationship. I say 'long' because after Jawa, I dated a guy for only about two months but I don't like to count him because he was such a loser. He had quit his job a week after we started dating and wouldn't even try to look for another. That turned me off. Plus he was pretentious; he actually believed he was good in bed and he wasn't. He was horrible. I didn't even tell him the real reason I broke up with him.

The next guy after him ended up being a pig. I found out he was married with a kid after I had already fallen for him, making it harder to leave him. But I eventually did. He was the richest guy I'd dated. He had a black custom Lexus sedan with an engine that could be started with the press of a button on its key fob, something I'd never seen before. He was one of the first to purchase the H1 Hummer when it first came out. He owned multiple properties all over the Bay area, and what actually attracted me to him was the power he had.

Once, after a long day together, it was very late and I was too sleepy to drive my own car back home, so he pulled out his cell phone, called one of his workers, waking him up, and told him to come and drive my car home. My house was over an hour away and the guy did so without question. That move impressed me, but it didn't hold water long enough to deal with him. We dated less than a year, though I'd prefer not to call it dating because he was a serial cheater.

I then met my college sweetheart, my second love after Jawa. He was handsome, intelligent, and passionate but above all, a leader amongst his peers. He had a quest for knowledge unlike anyone I had known. He questioned professors during class about why something was what it was and why it couldn't be something else. He questioned his peers on why they'd chosen certain majors, encouraging them not to take the 'easy road' with a degree in acting when they were smart enough to major in math or science, and they'd respond well to his suggestion. He was a great kisser too. That man knew the ins and outs of a woman's body. Just being around him and watching him interact with people was orgasmic.

But our love burned out after almost two years of dating. I guess he got scared that we were getting too serious. So one day he just stopped answering my calls for no reason, no fight, no argument. He just stopped. That, I'd say, was my first heartbreak. It was hard getting over him, but after a few months I did, when I met Sebastian.

Two

AGE 24 - 33

Waking up to his beautiful face every day for the past nine months in 2003 had been such a new experience for me. In all my 24 years of living, I had been used to sleeping alone, even when I was in relationships. I never had been one to spend the night at a boyfriend's house, or have them spend the night at my place. I believed in the saying, 'Distance makes the heart grow fonder', and I took it literally. It had been only three months since Sebastian and I got married and almost a year to the date when we met, but I knew he was my man the moment I laid eyes on him.

To be honest, I knew it the moment he hugged me after we had dinner together for the first time and he casually held me by the small of my back. The way he held me felt right, like 'home', like he was meant to hold me. Being half-Nigerian and half-American and having only dated American guys in the past, and now being with a Nigerian, I felt like I'd found someone who 'understood' me. Sebastian was twenty-nine-years old, 6 feet 4, with dark and evenly toned skin, perfectly white teeth, a smile that lit up a room, and a muscle toned body. He was born and raised in Nigeria and has one of the deepest accents I had ever heard. His voice was deep, smooth and sexy as hell. He also had a sincerity about him that was so unique and refreshing, and a natural charisma about him to boot.

"Good morning, beautiful" Sebastian said to me the second I opened my eyes lying next to him in bed. It couldn't have been past 5 a.m. and he looked like he had been awake for a while. "What were you dreaming about?" he asked.

"Nothing…nothing I can remember." I blushed knowing that he must have been staring at me as I slept. Ugh, that was awkward; I thought to myself: *If I were white, I would be beet-red right now.* "Why are you up so early? Couldn't sleep?" I asked him.

"I wasn't dreaming about you when I was asleep and I missed you, so I woke up, making sure you were still here. I don't like missing you."

My goodness, I thought, *he still says the most beautiful things to me even after we're married.* He began to run his hands down my back, grabbed my butt and gently pulled me towards him. He kissed my forehead lightly, then went down to my nose and kissed it; he fervently kissed me, turned me on my back, then kissed my neck and the middle of my chest, moved over to my right breast and softly sucked on my nipple, crossed over to my left nipple and lightly sucked on it and went down to my navel and gave it a quick lick; then he went down and kissed the creases between my thighs, lifted both my legs up and spread them open. He stopped and looked at me with a boyish smile, and just as soon, enclosed his face between my legs. The sensation never got old no matter how many times we made love. Sebastian had become a *master* at knowing my body and my hot-spots. My body exploded with exhilaration and he knew that was the moment I liked for him to put himself inside me. He slightly lifted me up by my waist, pushing more of him in me, and I began to moan.

"This woman, I love you so much," Sebastian said

as we made love. "I don't think I can ever get tired of making love to you, your body is so sweet."

"Mmmmmm…and it's all yours," I murmured as I turned on my stomach and he entered me from behind gently moving in and out of me. We made love till the sun beamed through the curtains. I had married my perfect man. He still had a yearning for me, and that turned me on.

Sebastian and I spent a lot of our time together talking about our future and his upbringing. We always had, even before we got married. But somehow, even though I had spoken with him about my past relationships, we never really spoke about my upbringing. It wasn't because I was keeping it from him; it's just that most of our talks had just been about our future and what we both wanted. I knew about his past, his struggles, and such, and I just wanted to be there to support him and be the sounding board he needed to vent any and all his frustrations. But somehow I never opened up to him or anyone else other than my two sisters about any emotional struggles I had and lucky for me, I didn't have a husband who pried or maybe he just didn't think to ask. Either way, it worked for me.

I had met Sebastian a year earlier while shopping at a small organic food store in Berkeley, California. It was a cool summer day and people were walking to their local farmers and flea markets, and were out on their bicycles. I had on a simple pair of fitted ankle-cropped blue jeans, a fitted white shirt and no make-up. I wore my hair curly and shoulder-length. I was walking up an aisle with my hand-held shopping basket and he, in a nice gray suit, was walking in the other direction. He looked like he just needed to pick up one item as he didn't have a basket in his hand. We quickly gazed at each other and he gave me a quirky smile. I just as quickly turned my face away, bashfully.

I walked to the other aisle and he came strolling behind me; I could feel him staring at me from behind, but I was still too shy to turn around. Feeling him close behind me, he quickly passed me, almost brushing my shoulder. He kept walking past me without uttering a word. He walked towards the check-out and began conversing with the guy at the register-Zack, the store owner.

I had known Zack for years. He was originally from Zimbabwe. He had mentioned to me in the past that he had traveled and lived in Nigeria and other African countries, and he knew some Nigerian languages. He and Sebastian were whispering to each other. Zack glanced over at me, and they both smiled at each other as if they had exchanged a secret. Sebastian walked out of the store before I reached the register, but not before he took one more look in my direction and gave me another smooth smile. When I reached the register, Zack had a boyish smile in silence as he rang up my items. "Someone's having a happy day," I said to him, hoping he'd open up to me about what he was discussing with the strange-beautiful man who had just left. "Why so happy?"

"Oma! Oma! Oma! You know, your parents named you well. You know what your name means, right?" he asked me, still smiling. Zack had a nice, soft, unfamiliar African accent; it seemed to be a mixture of French with an African base to it, and British English.

"Yes," I said. "Beautiful."

His smile got wider as he began to bag my items. "That's right! Beautiful! And I don't think you know how powerful your beauty is sometimes. Do you know how many men have asked me about you every time you come to my store? They are always asking me if you're married, if you are single, if you're in a relationship. And usually I don't tell you about them because some of them have been useless men, either married or ugly or…just useless. Not good enough for my sister."

Zack had always been a straight-talking, no-holds-barred kind of man as long as I'd known him. He handed me my first bag and I continued to let him speak, feeling humbled that he considered me his sister. "Well, this guy who just left…" He paused as his started to smile again and he shook his head, leaving me more curious, waiting to hear about this guy. "This one….let me just say, he is the one for you!" I smiled and looked away towards the door, as other customers walked in.

"Why? Why do you say he's the one?" I asked.

"Anyway," he continued, "that's it. Here's your other bag. Don't worry about the bill; that guy paid for it. And he told me to never let you pay me for anything from this store again, that any time you shop here, just put it on his credit card, no matter how much."

What? I thought, *how could a man who doesn't even know my name, let alone if I am even interested do such a thing for me?* I didn't know whether to be offended or impressed. I didn't want to feel like I owed him anything when I saw him, but I was also impressed by such a risky gesture, because he didn't come off as looking wealthy enough to leave his credit card open like that.

"What's his name?" I asked, trying to sound indifferent so as to keep my composure as I was sure

Zack would definitely tell him my reaction when they spoke again.

"Sebastian," Zack said.

"Well, you tell Mr. Sebastian when you see him next, 'Thank you, but no thanks.' If he wants my attention, he'll have to come a lot stronger than this." I said with a smile and started to hand my debit card to Zack to pay for my items.

"No, no, Ms. Oma, I cannot take it. I already charged his credit card for up to $400, and he told me if your bill came to be over that amount, to call him and he'll come back down and cover it."

"What was my total, Zack?" I asked, trying to stay straight-faced. Zack just shook his head. "I cannot double-charge, Ms. Oma. It's ok. I will tell him that you don't want to charge it again after this. But expect to see him again because he says he will come here every day around this time and wait to see if you will come back again. Maybe you can tell him yourself then?" Zack said hinting that maybe I should come by tomorrow.

"Ok, Zack. Thank you. We'll see you *soon* then," I replied.

I didn't show up for the next couple of days so I wouldn't come off as being awed, plus I wanted him to get curious and maybe anxious as to why I hadn't come by yet. I showed up on the third day and there he was, standing outside the store. I was sure he would have given up by now or that he'd be inside the store talking with Zack while waiting. I walked up to him as he lifted up from the wall he'd been leaning on. He looked more casual today than he had three days ago when he was in a suit. He had on blue jeans and a simple white T-shirt, and a black beanie covering his head. "Hello, Oma!" He said my name as if he had met me before, but I knew Zack must have told him my name.

"Hello, Sebastian," I said, letting him know I knew who he was, too.

"You finally decided to show up today?" Sebastian said with a coy smile, exposing a beautiful set of white, evenly aligned teeth. Hmmm, nothing like a man with a beautiful smile; it was definitely one of my favorite features in a man.

"I did. After you practically summoned me here with your grandiose offer," I said, smiling, trying not to expose how nervous I was.

"Are you free tonight, Oma? I'd like to take you out if you don't mind."

I looked down briefly trying to find the right words, and then looked back into his beautiful brown eyes. "I may be free," I said.

"When might be a good time for you?" he asked softly.

"Seven…seven p.m. will be ok," I said timidly.

"May I have your number, so I can call you later to get your address?" he asked.

I felt like saying something smart like, "What? You don't already have my number?" But the way he spoke to me was genuine and simple and I wanted to keep it like that. I reached into my purse and handed him one of my new business cards; I had started a party planner business that was only a few months old and it felt good to have a business card I could hand out. Sebastian took the card from me, all the while staring at me; he didn't take his eyes off me the whole time. It was quite an enticing feeling.

I found it difficult to find the right outfit to wear that evening. This was not a problem I usually had. I wasn't sure where Sebastian was taking me on our first date and I didn't want to over-dress or under-dress. After several dress changes, I decided on my favorite dress at the time, a long, body-hugging black and brown dress that was low-cut in the back; it was simple but elegant. In that moment, I appreciated having my body type; five feet, ten inches tall, slim and toned which helped. At least I thought so.

The doorbell rang. It was Sebastian; he showed up right on time at seven o'clock. He wore a pair of black jeans, a dark blazer over a simple white T-shirt and a pair of nice black loafers. "Wow! This girl you're fine oh!" Sebastian said in a cute Nigerian slang.

He was so adorable. His Nigerian accent came out strong, and he had a huge smile on his face, and was taking steps back and forth appearing to be truly in awe of me. His honesty was refreshing because none of my past boyfriends had made me feel so beautiful just by their reaction to seeing me. Sebastian didn't show up with flowers, but after his reaction, that was quickly forgiven.

"Thank you," I said. "You look good, too, Sebastian. Your shoes are nice."

"I know," he said jokingly. "Don't you know I'm a guy-man?!" (A man with style) he continued, and we both chuckled. He gained an extra point when he opened the car door of his Jeep Cherokee for me, and asked if I was comfortable when he got in. We went to an upscale Korean restaurant in downtown Oakland. I liked that our date was turning out to be different than my traditional date destinations of Chinese or franchise restaurants. "Have you been here before?" he asked as he opened the door of the restaurant for me.

"No, I haven't. It's really nice, how did you find this place?" Before he could answer, the restaurant host led us to our table in a quiet corner where Sebastian held my chair as I sat.

He then continued. "I come here sometimes. I lived in South Korea for over four years before I came to the U.S., and for the first few weeks I didn't eat their food because I didn't like it. One day, hunger struck me so hard, I finally ate their food and fell in love with it."

I laughed at his comment, fully understanding the power of hunger. I was genuinely impressed that he had lived in another country other than Nigerian and America.

"Hello, welcome to Jong Ga House. May I start you off with anything to drink?" a petite female server asked as Sebastian and I were mid-laugh. Sebastian then proceeded to place his order in Korean, which initially took the waitress aback. They carried on a brief conversation in Korean and I could gather from their dialogue that she was asking him where in Korea he lived and for how long. I could also tell he was happy to elaborate. While they conversed, I knew then why he picked that restaurant; he wanted to show-off his multilingual skills.

I quietly chuckled; it could have easily gone the other way for me, but he didn't come across as pretentious, I could tell he was truly just trying to win me over. It worked. The dinner date went very well, and our chemistry seemed to flow effortlessly. We sat and talked for almost three hours at the restaurant, about our likes and places we'd both traveled, and we found that we had quite a bit in common. We knew some of the same people in the Nigerian community, which surprised him. "You know him?" Sebastian exclaimed.

"Christopher?" I asked. "Yes, he used to be my father's best friend. They were very close many years back when my father first came to this country."

"Wow, it's a small world." It was nice to share a commonality with him. "Are you ready to go? We've been here for a while. You want to go somewhere to get some dessert?" Sebastian asked.

"Oh, no! I'm stuffed." We got up to leave, and as I was getting up, Sebastian came right in front of me, briefly stared at me, and leaned in and gave me a soft kiss on my lips. It was a nice and gentle kiss, and it didn't feel inappropriate. I felt like I was already his and he was mine. We took a slow walk back to his car, enjoying the cool evening breeze.

As we reached his car and he opened my door, I turned and said to him, "I enjoyed myself this evening, Sebastian."

He looked at me and smiled. "I enjoyed myself, too, Oma." Our drive back to my apartment was a bit quiet, but not in a bad way. Every so often, he looked in my direction and smiled and then turned away again as he drove. He seemed suddenly nervous. I felt like he was trying to say something but was struggling to get it out. "Oma, I really like you. And I'd really like to see you again. I don't know if you're free tomorrow?" he finally asked, uncertain of my reply. He was so cute, and endearing.

"I like you, too, Sebastian, and yes, I'm free tomorrow. I'd like it if we went out again," I said softly.

"Ok. Cool, cool…I'll call you tomorrow and see what time."

Sebastian and I went out practically every day after that for the next few months, and each time we went out we went somewhere new (besides going for walks around one of my favorite lakes). During our third month of dating, I heard from my dad's younger brother, Uncle Henrys, a respected cardiovascular surgeon, the 'rich' uncle in my family, and also quite private. So whenever we saw or heard from him, it was almost like seeing a celebrity. I believe he had a soft spot for me in his heart because not only did he believe in my capabilities, he showed it. He referred me to one of his fellow colleagues whose daughter was getting married in another state. He had referred to me as "The party planner to hire!" and they did indeed contact me. They were a wealthy family who sought a posh winter wedding in Atlanta and they said they had heard great things about my company from Dr. Banufo, my uncle, who, I must add, hadn't told them we were related, to help me appear more professional.

I was gone for a full week, the longest I had been away from Sebastian since we had met. We tried to speak on the phone every day, but I was so consumed with work, trying to find the perfect vendors in a different state that met my standards, that I didn't always have the time to talk on the phone with Sebastian.

It was about 7 p.m. when I got back from my trip. Sebastian picked me up from the airport, and we embraced each other like we hadn't seen each other in years. I had missed him so much; my heart ached just seeing him again. We kissed and he lifted me off the ground as he twirled me around hugging me. "Baby, I missed you so much!" he said.

"I missed you, too, love." I said.

"You hungry?" he asked. "Because I am starving! I haven't eaten all day because I was so excited you were coming back I didn't want to eat without you."

"No, I'm not really hungry; I'm just exhausted from this trip. This event might have been my highest paid event, but, boy, did they make sure I earned every penny. Rich people are very hard to please. But I'm just glad I was able to pull it all off and everyone was happy in the end," I said as we started walking towards the parking garage.

Sebastian suddenly changed the subject and said, "I have a surprise!"

"What?" Anxious to hear what the surprise was, I waited. "Beep beep." He pressed a key-fob and it opened a new Silver BMW "Oh my God, Sebastian! This is beautiful! When did you get this?" I asked as he opened my door and let me get in. He put my bags in the trunk and came around to the driver's side.

"Yesterday. I needed to change that Jeep; it has tried," he said.

"Well congratulations, babe, you deserve it. It looks good on you." I caressed his cheek and began to rub his neck and chest. "How fast can it drive us home?" I teased, hoping my hint of sex would override his hunger for food. All I wanted to do was go home, get in my bathtub, take a quiet bath, make love to my man and lie in bed together and fall asleep. Going out to eat was nowhere in my plans.

"Oma, honey, please I haven't eaten, can we at least quickly stop somewhere to eat? For me?"

Sebastian looked at me, making a sad puppy dog face. I laughed at how cute he looked. "Of course, babe...no problem."

Sebastian drove us into the city, to a restaurant we hadn't been to before; we walked in and "SURPRISE!" All my family members and friends were there. Ada, Uche, my cousins on both my mom's and dad's sides, my friends, Sebastian's friends and family. I screamed as the sudden fright of the surprise was totally unexpected. It wasn't my birthday, it was a normal Thursday evening and I didn't know what exactly the surprise was about. As I was busy trying to figure all this out in the short span of seconds, I turned to Sebastian to ask him what was going on, and I noticed he was on one knee behind me, holding open a black ring box with two sets of rings. "Oma, I love you so much. You have brought me so much joy these past few months. Yes, I know we've only been dating for three months, but I know I've found my true love. You are smart, kind, generous, a happy person, hard-working, a great cook, you have the body of a goddess and to top it all, you're drop-dead-gorgeous! How did I get so lucky to have someone like you love me? Oma, I LOVE YOU...you are my world and I want to spend the rest of my life with you. Please, Oma, will you marry me?"

For the first time in my life I was totally surprised. I started to tear up. I held my face in my hands and began to nod my head before I could even speak. "Yes...yes, Sebastian!" I replied behind tears of joy. Sebastian placed the rings on my finger. His hands were trembling a bit and I could tell he was nervous. He then got up from his knee, held my face with both of his hands, and kissed me ever so softly on my lips. Everyone started to clap and scream with excitement. "SHE SAID YES, YA'LL!!" Sebastian yelled, restating the obvious with a loud shout and everyone screamed with excitement again and clapped some more. In the midst of the celebration Sebastian whispered to me "Will you accept the 'be my wife' as well?"

Huh? I was confused at what he was saying. "The 'be my wife'?" I repeated.

"The BMW. I got it for you as part of this marriage proposal," he said.

"No way!?" I said in disbelief, I had never heard a BMW referred to like that before and I loved it. "Are you serious?" I asked Sebastian, making sure he wasn't just pulling my leg because that was a beautiful new car and it really did look good on him. I never imagined I would be the one driving it.

"Yes. It's yours, I don't want you driving in that bucket you call a car anymore," he teased about the Acura Legend I drove and was actually quite fond of.

"Bucket? Yeah, right, my car is awesome, buddy," I said playfully. "I can't believe you're giving me the BMW."

"I wanted to get you a brand new one, but they weren't giving me a good deal for my Jeep at the dealership with the new ones, so I took the pre-owned one, but it's still practically new," Sebastian said as if apologetic he hadn't bought me the new one. Was he kidding?

"Babe? The car is perfect. I love it. Thank you!" I kissed him.

Within six months, we were married in court and planned to have our traditional wedding in Nigeria within the next year.

Three

AGE 24 - 33

The following year, both our families were ecstatic about our upcoming traditional wedding being held at my paternal grandfather's house in the village. I flew back to Nigeria after almost a nine-year absence. Though we stayed in touch via telephone and letters, I hadn't seen my little brothers Christian Jr. and Nnamdi since they were babies. I looked forward to seeing many relatives again.

I arrived in Nigeria without Sebastian because he needed to finish up on some business before he could leave, so I had a couple of free days before Sebastian was scheduled to arrive. I used that opportunity to visit with Uncle BM, Aunty Teri, my cousins, Chisom and Alex. They were such a joy to see. They were always so protective of me and they hadn't changed. We reminisced, ate and told stories of the cultural differences between America and Nigeria. The next day, Alex took me to visit my brothers at their auntie's house. They met us outside the gate of the house, and we embraced on sight. "My goodness, Junior! Nnamdi! Look how big you guys are now!" I exclaimed. I was elated to see them again. They both had grown quite tall; Nnamdi had also grown bigger horizontally. "Nnamdi, look at that belly. What have you been eating? Have you left any food for your brother?" I teased.

"Abeg, leave me jare (*please leave me alone*). I like chocolate too much. Speaking of chocolate, did you bring me some?" Nnamdi asked anxiously.

"Nnamdi! Ah ah! Can she come inside? She just got here and you haven't even asked her if she's hungry or if you can offer her anything to drink. Na wa fo you oh! (*you're something else*)," Junior jokingly said to Nnamdi in my defense as we all walked into the house.

We met their aunt (Floressa's younger sister) at the door, and she welcomed me with a warm embrace.

"Oma! How are you? You're looking quite grown and beautiful." Aunty Marie had always spoken so elegantly, as if raised by royalty, she and Floressa had that same sophisticated quality.

"Thank you, Aunty. How is Richard?" I said, referring to her son whom I had grown up with when I lived in Nigeria.

"Richard is great. Right now he's in boarding school in England. I'll be sure to send him your love," Aunty Marie said gracefully.

I could tell she wanted me to know *her* son was also overseas and doing quite well. "Oh, that's great. It's good to see you again, Aunty. Your home is lovely," I complimented her as she led us into the living room. The room exuded sophistication as if to force upon any visitor the fact that she was classy. There was a massive, gold-framed mirror behind a fully stocked mini-bar, a 40 inch-television set, which was quite big for anyone living in Nigeria, two cream-colored, leather couches with dark brown, wooden head frames, and a round, glass coffee table in the center.

"Ester!" Marie called for her house-girl.

"Yes, Mom!" Ester called from the kitchen, running into the living room.

"We have guests. Please be sure to give them

whatever they want. I'll be leaving shortly," Aunty Marie instructed.

"Yes, Mom," Ester replied. Ester joined us. "Good afternoon, ma! What can I get for you?"

"Just a glass of water is fine," I said.

"Gimme Malta," Alex quickly added before Ester got to him.

"Ester, make sure it's very cold, oh! You know this is my sister and she just came from America, and she's not used to drinking hot water!" Nnamdi said, causing all of us to burst out into harmonious laughter. Nnamdi was such a clown and I loved that about him.

"Thank you, Ester," I said as she walked off to get the drinks. "So, are you guys coming to my wedding?" I asked my brothers.

"Ah, no oh!" Nnamdi responded.

"Why?" I asked, disappointed.

"We just can't go. Something about Daddy paying for our transportation there and for our hotel and all," Junior said, almost as if to prevent Nnamdi from saying much else. I knew there had been some issue with Dad and Mommy Floressa about the care of the boys since he had remarried, but I didn't know the depth of it.

"If transportation is the problem, Sebastian is supposed to be here by tomorrow; you guys can come with us and we can get you a hotel room," I said, hoping that would resolve the issue.

"Oma, it's already too late. It's ok. You know we love you and want to be there, but there's nothing we can do about it now. You guys are leaving tomorrow morning and it's already past 2 p.m. We can't go," Junior said, trying to sound unaffected from any hurt he might have been feeling.

I decided to leave the issue alone and change the subject. "Ok, can you guys at least come with me today to my hotel? Let's go swimming!"

Nnamdi shot out of his seat with an exhilaration he clearly couldn't contain. "Swimming? 'Ol boy, now you're talking! Junior, come, let us go and get our swimming suits jare. If we can't go and enjoy my sister's wedding, we're at least going to enjoy today!" Nnamdi said to Junior and they both sprinted off to their rooms to pack a bag.

I spent the rest of the day with my brothers and cousins, Alex and Chisom, at the Sheraton Hotel in Lagos poolside. We ate Suya (grilled spicy meat on a stick usually served with red onions wrapped in newspaper), had drinks and enjoyed lots and lots of laughs.

Sebastian came in the following day, and we set off

towards the East where our villages were to prepare for our wedding that was to be in two days. When we arrived and had settled in, we saw our plans begin to take shape as the wedding day drew nearer.

The night before our wedding, Sebastian put me and some of my family and friends up in the best hotel in my village and took off with his brother and uncle to his village. I prayed that he would have a safe trip back to his village because the roads were so bad and dangerous. I dreaded him leaving. Nothing but fear of losing him to armed robbers or a car accident stayed on my mind until he had called me to let me know he got in safely. Best call ever!

December 27, 2005: We had pulled out all the stops. I had two dress changes that day. My first dress was a long cannery yellow traditional laced dress with a ruby red beaded lace, overlapping the bottom of the dress with a short train and around the trim at the top of the dress. The second outfit was a bright gold top and skirt with matching head-tie. The native red beads my father gave me hung from my neck and on each arm and I held a uniquely designed yellow feathered fan in my hand. Oh, and Sebastian was stunning too.

We had a red carpet, a cake shaped in the form of a calabash (a traditional container used to hold palm wine, a local drink), loads of food and drinks - enough to feed the village - as well as lavish souvenirs; the Bible on CD, cups, flashlights, handheld fans, pens, and so much more. We had two different types of entertainment: a band with a lead singer, bass player, and dancers and one of the best local drummers come from Sebastian's village who played as Sebastian and all his family members came into my village. The two hundred guests included my family village king, respected chiefs and elders of our and surrounding villages, a few Nigerian political officials, and guests that flew in from the U.S, the United Kingdom, Canada, and across Nigeria. My grandfather's compound was overflowing with guests.

As Sebastian and I danced our first dance, he brought out folds and folds of one-dollar bills and showered me with an endless rain of money. The whole community was in absolute awe as they weren't used to seeing the dollar currency being thrown around in such amounts before. It was a beautiful and fun-filled event, and I was at my happiest.

AGE 4 - 13

It was 1991 when I met my mother Denise for the first time since I was two years old. We met her at a police station in San Pablo California. I was twelve years old, and it had been ten years since she last saw my sisters and me. But leading up to our first meeting with our mom, Dad had just brought Uche and me to the U.S from Nigeria to stay with him and our stepmom Floressa. Ada couldn't come with us at that time because she had to finish secondary school, and she still had a few months left before graduation. Ada, still in Nigeria, had written Mommy a letter telling her Uche and I were in the U.S, and asked if she would drop by to see us if she had the time.

Ada didn't know that we had actually been kidnapped by Dad ten years earlier, but, like any normal 12, 13, and 14 year-olds, we just wanted to meet our mom and see what she was like, and if she missed us. We later found out that when Mom got the letter and found out we were in the States, she called the police to tell them we were back in the U.S. Police officers showed up at our San Pablo apartment, took Uche and me, and a warrant for arrest was put on our father. Well, I guess it might help if I explain how we got to Nigeria in the first place.

AGE 15 - 19

On a gloomy Saturday afternoon in November, 1998, I was nineteen years old. I went to visit Mom in her little two-bedroom apartment in Union City, California.

"Omaaaaa! My baby! How are you? Oh my goodness, you look so beautiful, sweetheart! You always look beautiful!" Mom always greeted me with the sweetest compliments in the most expressive way. "How've you been? How's school?"

I'd smiled with warmth in my heart that she could exude such love for a child she didn't get to raise. "I've been good, Mom! Thanks. And school's going well, too! How've you been, Mom? You look like you've added a few more teacups since I last saw you." We both looked around at her display of teacups and puzzles hanging on the wall.

"Yeah," Mom said as she blushed over her collection. She had a love for teacups and had a slew of different types of teacups all over her living room and kitchenette area. She had made us some tea and biscuits, and it was quite a decision which teacups to use that day, but we soon agreed on a pink and white flowered teacup set. "I saw this one..." she held up the pink and white teacup in her hand "...in this small store I was walking past and it was on sale! Ain't it just the cutest? I love it!" Mom got excited over the littlest things and I loved that about her; it didn't take a lot to please her.

"It's gorgeous, Mom! Really cute!" I complimented her, knowing she was so proud of herself for finding it.

"Are you still seeing your guy friend I met some time ago?" Mom asked trying to catch up with me since our last visit. It had been some months since I last saw Mom, and it wasn't unusual not to see each other for months at a time.

"No, Mom. I'm not with that guy anymore." I blushed over her question. I wasn't always comfortable talking to Mom about guys because I knew it was a touchy subject for her. Somehow it always led to her painful past with Dad. "I'm seeing someone else right now. We're both in the same school. He's nice and all, but from now on, I'll only have you meet guys who have earned the privilege of meeting my mom," I said and she smiled.

"That's good, sweetheart, they definitely have to earn meeting me," Mom said, restating my statement as if to tell me what to do from now on. I went with it. We engaged in small talk for some time and of course the conversation soon turned to Mom's beginnings with Dad.

"How did you know Dad was the one for you at that time Mom?" I enjoyed talking about their beginnings because each time, she shared a new experience she had with him. We had some crackers with our tea and we began to reminisce on her times with Dad.

"Oma, your dad was some kinda man!" she said with the biggest smile on her face. I could tell she loved telling me about times she knew so much about and I knew little to nothing about because it brought us a little closer. Mom had missed out on ten years of our lives, but it wasn't by choice. She enjoyed any moment she had the opportunity to bridge some of that gap in those missed years.

"Really? How did you guys meet?" I asked anxiously. She eagerly began to tell me the story. "Well, I was dating your dad's friend at the time and one day, while I was sitting in the living room of my then boyfriend's apartment, in walks this tall, skinny, black as night man: your dad. He says hello to my boyfriend who was sitting next to me, who then introduces me to your dad. Then your dad sits down on the couch across from us and spends the rest of the visit staring at me, not taking his eyes off me the entire time. He had a fearless quality about him, not caring if his friend would have an issue with him for staring so hard."

Mom had a gaze in her eyes as she told the story, almost as if she were right back in that exact moment. Mom never dated any man after Dad, and she never remarried. She had a sadness about her that never really went away, or maybe just showed up when I came around because my presence triggered the bad memories. Not quite sure.

"So, what happened next?" I asked intently at the edge of my seat, waiting to hear the rest of the story.

"He soon started to pursue me every time he saw me and finally, one day wooed me into leaving his friend for him! Can you imagine?" she said, giggling like a young schoolgirl. It was nice seeing Mom laughing and smiling. "Your dad was a pilot at that time and on our first date, he took me on a plane ride in a single-engine plane around the bay and I fell instantly in love with him. I'd never met any man, let alone a black man in those days, so in control and confident. I knew I was going to marry him."

Mom and I talked for a long time about her and Dad's dating days and how they got married and started a family. Dad came from a "well off" family, one would say; at the time, his parents were sending money from Nigeria to the U.S to pay his school fees and financially support him, and Mom's family had a low-to-average

49

income because her father was the sole bread-winner in her family of seven children and her mother. "So, Mom, did you and Dad always want four kids? Or how did we all come about?" I asked, curious to know how my sisters and I were all a year apart and my little brother Jean-Pierre (JP) ended up being four years apart from me.

"Well, we had Ada first and your dad was somewhat pleased because he really wanted a boy, but nevertheless, he loved Ada and was happy with her." I knew what Mom meant by "somewhat pleased" because Dad, being a Nigerian and coming from a culture that believed having boys was a must and for Mom to be considered a true wife, a boy must be born. Mom continued "I was pregnant for three years straight trying for that boy. Uche came next, then you, and, by that time, your dad didn't even show up to the hospital anymore. He called the hospital after I had you asking what I had and when he found out you were a girl, he said ok and hung up the phone and never came to the hospital. Grandma took you and me home."

There was an uncomfortable silence after she said that. I knew she felt awkward having to tell me that and she knew I wouldn't be too pleased to hear it. But I didn't think too much into it. I brushed it off and Mom and I talked for hours more about her marriage and how she lost us. I wanted to know more. "How long were you guys married?" I asked Mom.

"Your dad and I were married for a little over ten years, and we did everything together."

Mom paused as she took a quick sip of her tea. Boy, could she tell stories.

Four

AGE 24 - 33

Sebastian and I had been married for a little over a year. He worked long hours at his office, sometimes eighteen-hour days. Sebastian ran one of the biggest dialysis centers in Danville, located in Northern California in. It had been a dream of his since he was a boy to open his own center one day, but he was taking his time learning all the ins and outs of the business, and he had been doing that for the past three years.

We used our down-time to go for walks around a lake that we lived near. We went for drives around the city looking at homes we dreamed of one day owning;

we went to new restaurants every time we went out to eat to try new foods and new ambiences. We thoroughly enjoyed each other's company like newly-weds. This was new ground for me yet again, because I had started leaving all my time and decision-making up to him to decide what to do next. I was enjoying having my man make the decisions for us - where we would eat, when we'd go for our walks - and it soon developed into where we would buy our first house, when we would start having children, and though it felt different, it still felt ok with me. I didn't feel like anything was being taken away from me; I didn't feel like I was being told what to do and when to do it.

I felt like this was how it was supposed to be. I had completely let go of my normal routine of being an independent woman who traveled three or more times a year prior to marriage, where I did what I wanted, when I wanted, to letting this man who obviously loved me take care of me. And that felt good; to not have to make a decision for once. It felt good to be cared for, it felt normal to let my man 'handle it' and handle it Sebastian did. He made decisions with ease and almost 90% of the time, he was right in those decisions he made. The few times he was wrong, well, those decisions were never drastic enough to alter our life. So I let him be 'the man' of our house.

We made the decision to be married for at least two years before starting a family, and I was happy he felt the same way I had always dreamed for myself; I had always wanted to spend at least the first two years alone with my husband before we started having kids.

AGE 15 - 19

I was at Mommy Denise's house and she was telling me about her relationship with Dad.

"We used to travel back and forth to Nigeria like it was taking a drive from Oakland to San Jose. It was so common back in those days going through the airport, which didn't even have security check-points. We just got on a plane as soon as we bought our ticket. I didn't like him going to Nigeria without me. I always wanted to be around him, so much so that even when I was pregnant with Uche, I induced labor to have her early just so I could go to Nigeria with your dad. I loved him so much, Oma!"

Mom's face went from smiling to straight-faced and an occasional grimace as she continued to tell me about her and Dad. "I remember wanting to please your dad so much. One day while we were in Nigeria, I wanted to surprise him, so I planned this elaborate dinner for him where I learned to cook his favorite soup. Ogbono soup, and I dressed up in a native wrapper and matching top - your Aunty Teri helped me with it.

Your dad came home drunk that evening. I gave him his meal and he said to me, 'What are you doing?

Why are you dressed like that? If I wanted a Nigerian wife, I would have married one.' He took everything I had cooked and threw it in the garbage." Mom paused and there was a brief silence. Then Mom told me something that I had never known about Dad. "We had a big argument that night and then he slapped me across my face and beat me."

I was startled to hear what Mom had told me. There I was, nineteen years old, and I had never experienced my father putting his hands on me or my sisters - not even once, our entire lives. I couldn't even remember a time I had ever seen my father get really angry at us.

"Mom!" I exclaimed. "But why? Was that the first time he ever hit you?" I asked, curious to know if that was a one-time thing and trying to find out if there was more to the story, because it just didn't fit the image I had of my father.

"No, Oma! Your dad used to beat me a lot. It really all started after I had Uche. I guess he really wanted that boy and he resented me for only having girls for him. By the time I had you, he just hated me and hated to be around me. He would cheat on me and even once had me meet one of the women he was sleeping with."

No no no…that couldn't be Dad! Not my dad. Why was she telling me this? It hurt too much to hear. What words were I supposed to say to my Mom after hearing this? "Why did you stay so long with him?"

She gave me a look that said 'you know why'. "Oma, I loved him and was afraid to lose him. But after I had you, I was starting to get tired of the insults, beatings, cheating, drinking - just everything. So, I filed for divorce and was granted custody of you girls when you were just two years old, Oma. Your dad got weekend visitation rights, and on his first weekend with you girls, when he came to pick you up, he asked me to pack some extra clothes for you girls because he was going to take you up to the mountains to see the snow and wanted a change of clothes for you girls in case you all got wet. So I did! I packed you extra clothes and was expecting you back Sunday evening. Sunday evening came and went and you guys were not back. I tried calling your dad, but he wasn't picking up his phone. I tried all night, and figured maybe you guys got stuck in the snow or traffic so I'd wait till the next morning." Mom told the story with tears welling up in her eyes. She was reliving this event again right before me.

"I knew something was wrong by morning. In fact, I had a feeling he had taken you girls to Nigeria."

"What made you think that?" I asked.

"Because I knew your dad and that's something he

would do, and I had that feeling in the pit of my stomach. I called your Aunty Nkechi, your dad's younger sister, and asked her if she'd heard from your dad and she told me that he had taken you girls to Nigeria and she thought I knew, I told her that I did not know he was doing that. Remember I told you buying a plane ticket in those days was as easy as buying a bus ticket, so I bought my ticket and hopped on the next plane to go get you girls back. When I got there, I knew I couldn't argue with him, nor could I be confrontational because things didn't work the same over there like it did here in America. When I got there, your dad had hidden your passports. In fact, he had his family hide them for him so I wouldn't find them and steal you girls back. I stayed with your dad for months trying to seduce him, hoping I could eventually persuade him to let me take you girls back, but he wouldn't budge. One day while he was out, and I was alone with you girls, I took you all, got in a taxi, went straight to the American Embassy and pleaded with them, telling them my story, that you girls were mine and my ex-husband stole you from me, and they said to me that you girls look like African children and they cannot let me take you without any documents to prove you were mine. I was so devastated and helpless; I wept all the way back to the house with you girls, knowing there was nothing I hadn't tried. Not too long after, I found out I was pregnant again. That's when I had to leave Nigeria. I didn't know what I was having at the time, but I was afraid that if I stayed with your father through that pregnancy, he would take the baby away, too. So I left you girls in Nigeria with your father and a few months later, I had Jean-Pierre."

Now I saw how we ended up in Nigeria and why Mom had not been around. "So when Dad found out Jean-Pierre was a boy, did he try to take him, too?" I asked, curious to know how Dad handled it when he finally got his boy.

"Well, no!" Mom said. "When I had Jean-Pierre, I made sure there was no connection between him and your father. I didn't put your father's name down as his father on his birth certificate and I gave him a French name and my last name so he couldn't touch him. Even male members of my church volunteered to be Jean-Pierre's personal security guards in case your dad tried to kidnap him, too. I made sure everyone who was around me knew my story and Jean-Pierre was protected."

Mom and I stared at each other in silence. I was in silent-shock mode after hearing what Mom had gone through all those years. She looked at me as if satisfied she was finally able to tell her side of the story. I had grown up not knowing the truth or what really happened between Mom and Dad. I wondered if Ada and Uche knew this, too, and didn't tell me, or would I be the one to tell them? Our tea had gotten cold and half-eaten crackers lay on our saucers.

"Mom! You are one strong woman. I can't believe you went through all that! I'm so sorry you had to endure that all alone."

I wiped tears away, as did Mom. We sat in silence a little while longer and Mom broke the silence with, "You hungry, sweetheart? I can make us something to eat."

Hungry? Was she kidding? "Gosh, no Mom. Far from it," I said with a weak smile on my face. I had just received a piece of my history that was not easy on the ears and heart, and for once, the last thing on my mind was food. Mom and I hadn't really ever been close. She had been diagnosed with clinical depression and taking medications for it and she had a strong sadness about her that I never really wanted to be around. But after visiting her, I saw where all that pain stemmed from.

However, Ada, Uche and I were here, back here in the United States; her girls whom she had lost for over ten years, had been back for over seven years and she didn't seem to want to be around us. She never called, never came to visit, and we'd only see her or speak with her if or when *we* called or visited. I didn't understand the disconnect there, either. I had thought maybe she would have wanted to be around us more, to get to know us more, but she didn't.

Once, Jean-Pierre and I were having an argument about this particular issue of Mom not caring to be around us, and also why he and Mom spent a lot of time at their church. At the time I didn't understand why Mom acted the way she did. Her church was her family and they always seemed to come first. Even after all those years of not seeing my sisters and me, she still couldn't put us first? She didn't try hard enough to come and see us and spend time with us; she never really called us. I just did not understand it and it made me mad.

JP, on the other hand, knew all too well about it and he tried to explain it to me. Once, he told me, in a confrontational kind of way, "Mom is sick, Oma! She cannot operate like a normal person. I grew up with Mom locking herself in her bedroom all day crying and I would be left alone in my room or the living room the rest of the day, and then she'd come out the next day smiling and acting like nothing had happened. Mom spent most of my life crying over losing you guys and I went through my whole childhood like that. The people in the church you're talking about are the ones who gave me the structure I have and took care of me. Mom just couldn't!"

I hadn't realized any of this before. It seemed that my little brother also went through his own difficulties growing up with Mom in that condition while also growing up without a father. I had never really stopped to think about that. I had a lot more compassion for JP after that day, and I think my realization of that helped us get a bit closer.

Five

AGE 24 - 33

It was 2005 and Sebastian and I were now venturing to buy our second home. We had been living in our first home for almost two years and now that we were planning on starting a family, we needed something bigger. We moved about an hour outside the main city inland to the suburbs. After all, that's what growing families did, right?

We bought the biggest house our money could afford at that time, which was a two-story 3300 square feet, four-bedroom four-bathroom house, with two living rooms, a chef's kitchen, a backyard with a waterfall fountain, and a three car garage on a cul-de-sac. There was a huge park with a baseball field, soccer field, and children's playground just two blocks from our home and we also lived in the best school district in the city. I initially didn't like the distance from the city as I was a city girl, but I soon grew to love this small quiet town of Livermore. We had our first child that fall, and it was a boy! Here we were, in our second home and it was just Sebastian, Sebastian Jr. and me, and we were the 'picture-perfect' family.

"Hey, sexy! How was your day?" Sebastian asked when he got home from work. I was a stay-at-home mom at this time, which wasn't really by choice because I was used to being out and about with a busy working schedule as a party planner for high-profile clients, but my son needed to spend his first year with Mom.

"Hi, honey! Not too bad. Did you miss me?" I asked him jokingly to see if I'd get a loving response.

Sebastian walked towards me where I sat on the kitchen table with Jr. in his high-chair and he kissed me on the lips, then pulled away ever so slightly. "I always miss you, babe." And he kissed me again. Then he went over to Junior. "Hey, son! You been taking care of your mom for Daddy?" he asked and kissed him on the head as Junior continued to play with the cereal on his high-chair table. "What's for dinner?" Sebastian asked as he walked towards the fridge and grabbed a box of juice.

"We still have some soup left over and rice and stew if you want. You want me to warm some up for you now?" I asked.

Sebastian stood at the refrigerator door looking into the fridge. "Na, maybe you can call your sister to see if she can watch Junior. Let's go out for dinner. After all, let us try and enjoy some of the money we're making. It's not the same food one has to be eating every day."

Hmmm, I loved it when he was in a cheerful mood and wanted to have alone time with me outside the house. It was sometimes boring being home alone with a child. The past few months, I had been feeling left out of the adult world. I didn't know anyone in this new town, no one I knew lived close enough for me to run over and visit, and none of my sisters or girlfriends had gotten married yet or had any kids, so I had no one to call whenever something 'new' happened with Junior.

Ada agreed to come help watch Junior for us, and she came over a couple of hours later, allowing Sebastian and me to have a much needed, way overdue date night. It was our first date night in over three months. I still had a bit of my baby weight on as I'd gained over fifty pounds with Junior and I'd lost about thirty-five pounds so far. Those last fifteen were stubborn ones for me. But I made it work anyway. I wore one of my favorite dresses, 'my little black dress'. It hugged my body and showed my figure in a way that brought a smile to my man's face. I always knew I looked good when Sebastian would smile at me after I got dressed. But these days he never said I looked nice, or ravishing or anything like that. He'd just smile, and I knew I looked good.

That night when we got back from our date, we made love like we hadn't in months; two months later, I found out I was pregnant with our second child. She was a girl!

AGE 4 - 13

Growing up in Nigeria was such a bittersweet experience; I believe Ada, Uche and my relationship was quite unique because of our experiences together. When we first moved there, we lived in a very small apartment in Akoka, a busy, boisterous, less-than-elegant neighborhood. The apartment housed Dad, his younger brother, Uncle BM, his wife Aunty Teri, their two-year-old daughter Chisom, and my sisters and me. It was a two-bedroom apartment with the bathroom outside of the unit, and a small living room area with one couch and a simple wooden table.

Dad and we girls stayed there for only a couple of months until Dad could save up enough money to get his own place. I have very few memories of Akoka because I was just three going on four years old at the time. But the smells and discomfort of living there, compared with where I had just come from in America, resonated with me. When we'd wake up in the morning, Aunty Teri would give us girls our baths outside, from a large washbasin in the publicly used compound. She then gave us breakfast of hot tea and bread, and sometimes a dish I was unfamiliar with called Akamu (a white, starchy, smooth, warm, custard-like meal usually mixed with sugar and milk for added flavor). I despised it. It had an aftertaste I didn't like and I threw it up several times. But we didn't have too many other options for meals at the time, so I soon got used to it after I got hungry enough.

After three or four months in Akoka, Dad moved with us girls to Aguda in early 1983. I had turned four, Ada was six and Uche five. Aguda was a much nicer area in those days, as compared to Akoka. Our apartment was in a gated housing area with two other buildings separating us from the busy street. We lived on the top floor of one of the four-story brown buildings, which was a big deal. Living on the top floor of any building in Nigeria constituted you as being 'rich' and of a 'higher class'. Our unit was a three-bedroom, two-bath apartment with a dining area. Dad bought a small grand piano and put it by the dining area, a dryer that was put in the bathroom in the hallway and one of those bulky color television sets with antennas in the living room. Some would say we were 'well off'.

Floressa came into the picture around this time. She was tall, stunning, and statuesque. She had a presence about her that no one could miss. She was always dressed in the best clothing, her nails were beautifully manicured, and when she walked into any room, people would stop, stare and admire her. She came around more often than usual and more often than the others. We became used to seeing her and some other women Dad was seeing off and on. She and Dad soon got married but I don't remember them having a wedding. Maybe they just got married in court, I don't quite remember. Anyway, she then stayed with us and we all were so happy and excited about that, because she was always so nice to us. She also enjoyed cooking and, boy, was she good at it. My dad was the happiest I'd seen him since I could remember. Floressa played games with us and made us fun, kid-friendly meals like meatballs (which was unusual for Nigeria), when we would all hang out together, she'd carry me a lot, help us with our hair, make sure we were neatly dressed each day and just laid lots of hugs and kisses on us. I knew this was what having a mom felt like because at that time I didn't remember my real mother anymore. I hadn't seen my mom in over two years and I no longer remembered that Floressa was not my real mother. As far as I knew at age four, Floressa was Mom and that's what we called her: "Mommy".

Dad started traveling a lot more to the U.S. so we

were mostly being cared for by house-boys and house-girls and our stepmom. Floressa was very picky about our house help; we went through so many of them I lost count after eight. She had once fired a house-girl she hired after just two days of working for us because she 'smelled bad'. She fired another one because she kept falling asleep while working (I guess she must have had a sleeping disorder), and countless others for various reasons.

There was one particular house boy she hired named Assi who was with us for a few months. Assi was a twenty-two year old man with a friendly-looking face and demeanor. He liked to laugh a lot and was very obedient to Floressa whenever she asked him to do anything. One could tell he really needed his job and wanted to keep it. His job was to wash the car, chauffeur Floressa and Dad around when they needed to go anywhere, and wash and iron the laundry. Assi was so nice to Ada, Uche and me. He was funny, took care of us even when he wasn't expected to, always gave us sweets, cookies and biscuits, and played games with us.

One afternoon, my sisters and I were playing with each other in the living room; Dad had traveled, and Floressa was out. Assi asked us girls to come into the guest bedroom and told us he wanted to play a game with us. He shut the door, then proceeded to lie on the bed. He pulled his pants down and his penis, fully erect, came popping out. He then said, "Let me show you guys something," and he maneuvered his penis to move around in circles without touching it. "Wow!" my sisters and I exclaimed. We were amazed at what we were seeing; I was full of wonder at how he did that, and without hands! That was so cool to me. After a few minutes, he then said to us, "Whichever one of you guys that can put this whole thing in your mouth, that person I will buy Fanta for!"

Oh cool I thought, I liked playing games and I wanted to win that Fanta. I loved Fanta! Ada went first, but she didn't even open her mouth fully, she just kissed the very top and pulled away. Boy, this was going to be an easy game to win I thought to myself. Uche went next and she got about halfway or so and took it out of her mouth. *I can beat that*, I thought. Then it was my turn. I put as much of him into my mouth as I could fit and remembered gagging a bit trying to win my Fanta.

"Very good, Oma!" he exclaimed. "Now use your tongue to touch it, too."

I didn't realize he wanted me to have my tongue lick it, too! *Ewwww* I thought. I had put him in my mouth, yes, but I dipped my tongue down as far as I could so I

71

wouldn't have to taste him. No. I shook my head as I pulled him out of my mouth. "I will vomit," I told him.

Oh oh! He looked upset. "Ok, then you can't have your Fanta." He pulled his pants back up and we all walked out. We didn't tell Floressa when she got back because I guess we hadn't realized the "game" we played was a bad one.

Dad came back home a few weeks later and, by that time, Assi had sexually assaulted us multiple times.

Dad usually liked to sit out on the balcony with his Gulder beer on a stool as he watched people go about their day. Sometimes I'd go out there with him and sit on his lap, and we'd watch the street in silence together, and sometimes I'd ask for things like soda or candy and he'd make it happen. Those were some of my most happiest times because I felt safe, and like I could be myself with him and he loved me regardless. I knew I was Daddy's little girl.

One day, Ada must have had enough of Assi and probably didn't know how to tell Dad what was happening without fear of reprimand. And going to Floressa was never an option, especially when it came to sensitive matters like this. We were all in the living room. Ada, and Uche were standing behind the sofa with Assi standing not too far from them, and I was sitting on one of the other sofa chairs watching TV. Dad was sitting out on the balcony as usual, drinking his beer and smoking his pipe. Ada said to me in a loud voice as if she had just come out of an argument, "Go and tell Daddy what Assi has been doing to us, Oma. Go now!"

"No no... I beg! Make una no do this to me! I Beg!" (*Please, I'm begging you guys, don't do this to me*). Assi began to shake and plead for me not to go, while Ada and Uche both started to wave their hands and motion their heads towards the balcony. I slowly started walking towards Dad while looking back over my shoulder to see if my sisters would tell me to come back. They didn't. I finally got to Dad.

"Dee-Dee!" This was the nickname my dad would call me, he said because I looked so much like my mother Denise.

"Daddy," I said with my head hanging down, afraid of what Daddy would do to me.

"Yes? What is it?" he asked.

I started to get nervous and I slowly let it out "...Assi...has been fucking us," I said quietly and under my breath, unaware that 'fucking' was a really bad word. I had heard Dad use it before, so it was a regular word for what two adults do to each other in my little mind.

"What did you say?" Dad asked, as he lowered his beer and brought his face closer to mine to hear me better.

"I said, Assi has been fucking us!"

Dad had a confused look on his face as he tried to decipher what I had just told him. "What do you mean he's been fucking you? How?" he asked as if to make sure I knew what the word meant.

"Like this…" I then motioned my lower body in a back and forth motion and I noticed Dad's eyes instantly turned red. I immediately thought he was mad at me, but then he must have seen the fear in my eyes.

"Ok, Oma, Daddy has heard you, okay?" He had caught himself and reassured me with a hug and motioned me back into the apartment. By the time I walked back in, Assi was gone. Dad walked in and asked Ada where Assi was and Ada said he ran away.

I'm not sure what happened after that, but Dad quickly got dressed and left. Later on that evening, Floressa took my sisters and me with her to meet Dad twenty minutes away in Ikate where Uncle BM, Aunty Teri and our cousins Chisom and Alex lived. My sisters and I really loved going there because we'd visit and play with our cousins and neighborhood kids. When we got there, Dad was with his brothers, neighborhood friends, about seven police officers and Assi. I remember one of the police officers tightly held the back of Assi's neck, while Assi's hands were handcuffed in front of him. My sisters and I were quickly sent off to go play with our cousins. I never knew what became of Assi after that. I just know it mustn't have been good.

Dad had to start traveling again; he used to travel all over the world back then, mostly to the U.S, and sometimes to China, Australia and some other countries whose names I couldn't pronounce at that time and wouldn't remember soon after he'd said where he was going. I was always sad seeing Dad travel a lot, but the best part was his return because he always brought us back lots of goodies like sweets, Hubba Bubba bubble gum, new shoes, clothes, watches, foods we'd never seen in Nigeria - it was great! "You girls be good now and Ada, make sure you look after your sisters, you hear? They are your baby sisters, ok?" Dad said to Ada as he held his bag to leave that evening.

"Yes, Daddy!" Ada would reply with a sad face.

Dad hugged us and was gone. Then the beatings grew worse.

I cannot recall the very first beating I got from Floressa. I can only remember that there were lots of them and I remember the warnings she used to give us, that if we ever told Daddy or anyone else that she was beating us, she would kill him and us. Boy, did we know she meant it, because everything she promised she'd do to us if we didn't behave, she did. Dad had started going for longer stretches than usual now that we had a 'mom' at home. He used to leave for only a couple of weeks at a time before he got married, but now he was gone months at a time.

Six

AGE 4 - 13

A little over a year later, I started to pee in my bed and Floressa hated that about me. Every morning I would wake up on a damp, urine-soaked bed and as soon as I felt it, fear would engulf me and I'd begin to tremble because since I had started peeing in the bed, Floressa's morning routine had been coming into our room first thing to check if I had peed in the bed, as if she were hopeful I had – and I certainly had. "Just look at you! Agbaiya! (*An insult, expressing one as immature for one's age*) So you didn't wake up and go and use the toilet like I told you to last night!" she'd say as she began to lunge at me. I whimpered and took a few steps back in fear of what was coming as I couldn't run away from her; that would have just been the worst thing to do.

She beat me mercilessly, hitting my head and back as I was scrunched over. "Stupid idiot! What is the matter with you? Eh? Are you not ashamed of yourself? Just look at your bed, do you see how you're making your whole room smell like a toilet? C'mon, pick up that mattress and take it out to your balcony now!" and she'd give a long hiss and walk out of the room calling after Ada and Uche to go take their baths.

Ada and Uche would walk out with their heads hanging low; I could tell they wanted to stay to comfort me and help me with my mattress, but they had to do as Floressa said. I was in pain from the beating and on some occasions the beating wasn't complete until I bled from my lip or nose, so the sores barely healed from the previous beatings causing them to reopen by the following morning.

I was small, still six years old, and carrying my full-size mattress out to our bedroom balcony to dry was always a battle for me. It took me forever to carry it and maneuver it around Uche's bed which was right next to the sliding door that led out to the balcony, but I made it. Other times, when Floressa was either not home or didn't come into our room to check, Ada and Uche would help me take the mattress out, not letting me help them. During those times, Ada almost always said, "Oma, you have to try and stop peeing in the bed."

I could tell what she was saying was more like a plea for me to try and stop the beatings she could not protect me from. I cannot remember my sisters and me getting into many fights with each other growing up; not physical ones at least. We grew up with so many beatings from our stepmom. There was nothing to disagree on most of the time.

I do know I loved to mimic Uche a lot, which she hated! If she did something, I'd do it, too. If she said something a certain way, I'd say it that exact same way next time. I figured it was the best thing to do because Floressa barely beat her, and I figured if I could just be a bit more like Uche, my beatings might be less. Uche was mostly quiet and she kept herself clean; her shoes and socks were also always so clean, she never got her hair or dress dirty. She had this self-comforting habit she had developed where she would rub her belly button with her finger and suck on her tongue. She did that most of the day every day and that was her way of 'getting away', I suppose, because she often had a dazed look as if somewhere far away; then she'd fall fast asleep sucking. I remember trying to do that, but I couldn't understand what comfort she got out of that; it just seemed like a boring habit to have, and I didn't understand what was so 'fun' about it. Ada, on the other hand, sucked her thumb for her comfort, and I just liked to play with my toys and play pretend. That was my comfort; it allowed me to escape from my reality, if only for moments at a time.

One cloudy day, it was about six o'clock in the evening and Floressa wasn't home. It was a weekend and that's when she went out to parties. She had already given birth to my first half brother Christian Jr. by then who was still a baby, so Floressa most likely had taken him to her mother's house to baby-sit. Uche, seven years old at the time, had her very first rebellious act and it was a big one, too, so much so that it had me and everyone there that day completely shocked, because again, she was usually the quiet one. We used to have different house-boys and house-girls in our home at different times, for various duties. One of the house boys that day decided upon himself to go into our refrigerator and take one of our dad's beers and drink it without permission. While he was drinking the beer Uche began confronting him for being so bold as to go into our fridge in the first place; she seemed more outspoken that day than she usually was. Uche tried everything to upset this house-boy and he seemed unfazed and Uche just didn't like it. She then said to the house-boy, "If you can drink my daddy's beer without permission, then me, too; I'm going to go and take one beer and drink it, too!"

The house-boy then tried to discourage Uche from drinking the beer, but Uche refused to listen to him. Ada tried her *I'm your older sister and you must listen to me* tone with her and Uche brushed her off without fear. Uche proceeded to drink the entire forty-ounce bottle of beer effortlessly; when Uche put her mind to anything, she never stopped till it was done. Ada went into our bedroom, and closed the door. I could tell she wanted nothing to do with what was going on. Then Uche opened a second bottle and finished that one as well; afterwards, she started slurring her words when she tried to speak. She was staggering about, and her eyes were red; she sat on the couch with her legs open, unlike a lady as Floressa had taught us to sit. When Uche was done with the second bottle, she staggered over to the fridge, got yet another bottle, opened the third bottle, and started drinking it. She only drank about a quarter of it and soon passed out, and on my bed, too.

I had just seen my older sister finish two and a half (well, almost half) full bottles. I was afraid of what Floressa would do to Uche if she came home right then. But God had mercy on all our poor little souls in that house that evening because Floressa didn't come back until the following day. I know if Floressa had seen what happened, the house-boy most likely would have been fired for drinking Dad's beer, Ada definitely would have been beaten for not stopping Uche, and I also would have gotten a beating (well, maybe just slapped across the face) for sitting and watching the whole thing happen and to warn me never to try such a thing; and Uche...well, Uche might have died from the beating she would have received. If we got serious beatings for minor things like getting our shoes dirty after playing, what would have become of Uche? We just couldn't afford to be bad children at all.

"Ewwww....Uche!! You vomited all over my pillow!" I pouted at Uche as she woke up the next morning looking like she was deathly ill.

"Sorry!" she said under her breath. Ada hurriedly took my pillow and pillowcase without saying a word to Uche and went to the bathroom to wash off the vomit, and hung the pillow case out on the balcony rails to dry. Uche somehow got over her hang-over that day without

Floressa noticing her, nor did she ever find out what took place the night before. Floressa stayed in her room with Junior most times since he was born, so she didn't seem to spend too much time noticing things that happened around the house as she usually did.

AGE 24 - 33

Sebastian's and my relationship as a married couple, of course, had its ups and downs, but lately I simply hadn't been getting as much attention from him as he used to give me. In fact, he outright ignored me most of the time now. In our first four years of marriage, Sebastian spoiled me with spur-of-the moment surprises like flowers on a Tuesday, dinners when I may have been too tired to cook, the usual birthday and Christmas presents, and so on.

But for some reason, within the last couple of years, his interest in me had basically faded. Maybe this was normal for relationships after being married for a long time, I told myself, trying to play down the concern I had. After all, we'd been married for over six years at this point, we had two children, and we'd hired a live-in nanny so I could return to work to assist with our growing bills. Besides, being a good mother to my babies Sebastian Jr. and Amaka was my main life's goal. Nothing of the experience I had with Floressa was ever going to resemble the experience I would have with my babies. I was beyond certain that I would by all means necessary prevent any physical abuse, verbal abuse, mental torture, sexual abuse, sexual assault, abandonment, dependent behaviors, homelessness, and bullying from happening to them. It may have seemed like 'over-kill' protection whenever I'd verbalize it to people, but it's far from that for me. I was a mother now and it was my duty to protect my children to the very best of my ability.

When Sebastian and I decided to hire a nanny, I hadn't realized the impact having one would have on my relationship with my kids. Because of Teresa, our nanny, my kids got the 'good' Mommy most of the time. When I got home from work, I had the luxury of extra time to rest a bit before honing in on homework, dinner, extra-curricular activities, or parent-teacher meetings. This was a luxury Mommy Floressa also had, but apparently it didn't make a difference in her child-rearing choices. With the exception of the parent-teacher meetings, if I happened to be too tired to do anything else, Teresa filled in those gaps and in the end I wasn't a frustrated mom, I wasn't yelling at the kids unnecessarily out of exhaustion and I got to be the fun-loving mom most times.

Prior to stabilizing with Teresa, I had gone through several nannies. I was overly cautious when interviewing potential live-in nannies and even still cautious after hiring them. I once fired a nanny who yelled too loudly at my kids; I didn't want them growing up thinking that was the only way to get a point across. I fired another who had a nonchalant response to Amaka when she had a food allergy. I was in school at that time and I received a telephone call from the nanny saying she had mistakenly given Amaka Cream of Wheat cereal with whole milk that was meant for Junior. She had tried to convince me that Amaka's facial swelling that resulted from the allergy was 'going down' and that she was ok. When I asked her to send me a picture of Amaka, my poor baby was unrecognizable and I was suddenly overcome with fear. I knew that internally her throat would soon start to swell up and obstruct her breathing, so I yelled at the nanny to give Amaka a shot with her Epi-pen and to call 911 immediately. I sped home from school while calling Sebastian at work to try and get home before I could.

The last nanny I had to let go of did a great job with the kids for about a year, but later, met a guy and started to bring him over to the house. I tried to be lenient with his visits because she was a good nanny and he appeared to be a nice guy and was occasionally helpful around the house. But when she asked if he could live with us, that was the big no-no. I could keep an eye on him when he visited and left, but I most certainly couldn't do so 24 hours a day. After all, pedophiles don't come with a *Beware* warning sign on their foreheads.

Going back to work felt like I had to start all over because after being off for about two and a half years, I had lost most of my vendors and had sent all my referrals to my competitors. I began despising Sebastian for not being as attentive as he used to be and I resented the fact that I felt needy as a wife, as that was never who I was used to being. I used the resentment I had towards my husband and threw it into work and exercise. After six months, I was back to planning several parties at once, making sure to secure at least one high-profile party every month, and in my downtime I used it to go running around the park down the street from our home. It was about a mile and a half around one time, so I would run three to four times around and if I was really stressed out and had extra time to burn, I ran five or six times around. I not only lost my second baby weight, but I was back to my pre-pregnancy weight and back to being busy with work.

Sebastian now seemed to be the one resenting me. However he didn't express his resentment the way I expressed mine. He shut me out most times; he'd come home and act like I was not even in the room, got dressed and leave without saying where he was going and what time he was coming back. We hadn't even had a fight about anything in particular; we just had a silent bitterness towards each other. If something was bothering him, I didn't stop to ask him, the same way he never stopped to ask me if anything was bothering me.

This was new ground for both of us; we had gone six years without treating each other this way. Something was definitely broken and neither one of us was willing to be the first to try to figure it out and 'fix it'. The good part about both of us throwing our time and energy into work for months was that we ended up earning double that year of what we had earned in previous years. The bad part about it was that it was changing the way we treated each other for the worse. We both had developed an 'I don't care attitude' towards one another and it was ruining our 'picture-perfect' life.

I was lying in bed one late afternoon while the kids were down for a nap, the nanny was out at the grocery store to pick up some food items, and Sebastian was also out. I began to reminisce about our wedding day. I remembered how nervous we both were saying "I do" at the altar. Sebastian had a bit of jokester in him and rather than saying "I do" when asked if he'd take me to be his wife, he shouted out, "Hell, yeah!" causing the few people there to burst out with laughter. Boy, those were the good ol' days, when Sebastian yearned for me. Now, I was self-reflecting to see if any part of me had changed; might it have been something I was doing or maybe stopped doing that had caused my marriage to get to where we were? I made a decision to initiate a conversation with Sebastian when he got home. I told myself to avoid bringing up the 'obvious' disconnect and to just stick to pleasantries and see where it took us. Sebastian got home almost as soon as I made that decision.

When I heard the garage door opening I sat up in bed, turned on the TV and waited for him to make it up to our room. "Hi, Honey!..." I said with a lump in my throat, because I knew that 'honey' wasn't a sincere 'honey'. "How was your day?"

Sebastian barely looked in my direction and said, "Fine." He put his keys away, took off his shoes, socks, shirt, and pants, and walked between the bedroom and master bath. He didn't reciprocate my question to ask how my day was.

I tried again. "I'm looking for something to watch on TV. Maybe we can order an On-Demand movie," I suggested, hoping he'd give a more than a one-word response. He ignored me. "Sebastian? I'm asking you a question. Or are you not interested in watching anything tonight?" I asked.

"Oma, I really don't know what it is you want. You can watch whatever it is you want to watch. There's nothing I want to watch; just knock yourself out," he said coldly as he took off his underwear and jumped into the shower.

My mind overflowed with questions and confusion as to why he thought he had the audacity to behave like I had been the one who had done anything wrong. I decided to hold my tongue and swallow any ounce of pride I had left to prevent any arguments.

Seven

AGE 4 - 13

It was early November 1986. Dad was back from one of his trips to the United States. I remember that particular night he got back because I had a bruised lip and was intent on Dad seeing it. Dad had unpacked one of his suitcases and given us all the goodies he had bought us: new tennis shoes, new clothes, different kinds of candies we'd never had before, and our favorite bubble gum.

After we had put all our new things away in our room, my sisters and I went to the living room where Dad was walking back from the kitchen after getting a beer from the fridge. He stopped behind the couch as we met him with hugs, and I climbed on the arm of the couch and was kneeling on it. Ada and Uche were on either side of him and we were all catching up with him about his trip, while Floressa was in their bedroom. She had just beaten me the night before; I don't remember what for and the beating had produced a cut on the inside of my lower lip from it and I wanted Dad to see it without me having to tell him. That way when he asked me what had happened to my lip, I would *HAVE* to tell him the truth, as Floressa had given me lots of beatings for lying.

So, as Dad was talking, I hung my lower lip out waiting for him to see it, but he kept missing it; I remember even trying to pout my lip out as I was talking and he still missed it. Ada, however, caught what I was doing and gently nudged me while slightly shaking her head for me to stop it. I knew then I had to stop. Otherwise I would have gotten into trouble with Ada later. Dad didn't get to see my bruised lip that day.

Almost a year later, Dad had an announcement. "You girls pack up all your clothes and things; we're moving!" Dad was in our bedroom on a Sunday morning. Ada had been sent to boarding school, so she wasn't there.

"Yay!" Uche and I screamed with excitement. "Is Mommy coming, too?" I asked excitedly, hoping we were leaving Floressa there in Aguda.

And Dad with a slightly confused look on his face said, "Of course! Don't you want her to come?"

"Yes, Daddy!" we both belted out, not wanting to show any signs of disappointment. Dad had finished building a house on Banufo Street in Ikate. It was a four-story, dark blue house with four-bedrooms, three and a half bathrooms, dining room, living room, long hallway and a balcony overlooking the street below where the people were almost tiny specks as compared to where we were.

We had all kinds of people in our apartment in Aguda that day helping us with the move from our rented apartment to our very own house in Ikate Surulere. Dad didn't have to physically help with the move at all; he paid people for that. So he went out with his friends and brothers to celebrate his new home while Floressa, who was pregnant with Nnamdi at the time, made sure the move was a successful transition.

Floressa had given both of us girls our duties to help with the move. One of my duties was to help with moving the vinyl records and arranging them neatly in our new living room under the record player. Somehow,

I mistakenly broke one of the records and to my misfortune, Floressa found out. "I'll deal with you later!" she said to me.

There went my heart rate, elevated, causing the oh-so-familiar lump in my throat again. I had heart palpitations the rest of the day and stayed quietly in my new room I would share with my sisters. I remember sitting on my already put together bed, with my head hanging low, wondering how I could have been so careless. I started to cry, fearing what was to come. I looked at my tears falling on my already dirty clothes. It was close to 5 p.m. and Floressa finally called me into what would be the guest bedroom; our house-girl was in there with her, and I believe she most likely was the one who told Floressa I had broken the record, but it wasn't unusual for the house help to tell their madam when we kids did anything wrong. Floressa was sitting on the bare bed in the room and the house-girl is standing next to her.

"Kneel down, my friend!" Floressa snapped. I knelt in front of her with a different kind of fear I hadn't quite experienced, because usually she'd just go in for the beatings and insults and walk away; I couldn't recall a time she had asked me to kneel down. Floressa lifted the broken record in her hand and showed it to me. "So you cannot even do anything without breaking something? Eh?" I hung my head down. "C'mon, look at me when I'm talking to you!" she belted out at me. "Now I'm going to teach you a new song. And anytime I'm coming home from now on, whenever you hear me start singing it, you will have a part to say and you must reply to me. You hear?"

"Yes, Mommy!" I replied, not fully understanding what she meant by 'a part to say' I was still confused at what was about to happen to me. Floressa then said, "When I say '**FOOD**' I want you to say '**I WILL EAT**'. When I say '**BOOK**' you will reply '**I DON'T KNOW**'. When I say '**EVERYTHING IN THE HOUSE**' I want you to say '**I WILL DESTROY**'.

When I say '**LIES**' I want you to say '**I WILL TELL**'. Do you hear me?"

"Yes, Mommy!" I replied, though again I didn't know what she wanted me to do. I was just waiting for my normal beating.

She began "**FOOD**!" I was quiet, waiting for more instructions. "Oma! Say 'I WILL EAT!'" she yelled.

"I will eat," I mumbled.

"No...shout it loud so I can hear. I want you to shout it loud whenever I'm coming up the stairs, I want to hear you shout it down to where I will be standing so

I can hear you. Do you understand me?"

"Yes, Mommy!"

"**FOOD**!" she belted out

"**I WILL EAT**!" I replied.

"Now I'll say, 'Book' and you say 'I don't know', you hear?" Floressa shouted, "**BOOK**!"

"**I DON'T KNOW**!" I shouted.

"When I say 'everything in the house', you will say 'I will destroy', ok? **EVERYTHING IN THE HOUSE!**" she yelled.

"**I WILL DESTROY**," I yelled out.

"**LIES**!" she shouted.

There was a silence because I wasn't sure what I was supposed to say, but I did know I had gotten a lot of beatings for lying so I belted out "**IS NOT GOOD**!"

She slapped me across the face with the broken record, and I fell from my knees to the floor. "C'mon, get up, stupid girl!" she shouted. "I will tell," she said.

Oh my goodness, she's going to tell Dad on me, I thought. I didn't want to get in any more trouble, especially with Dad.

"Lies!" she belted out again…and still a pause from me as I still wasn't sure what she wanted me to say, so again I murmured, "Is not good?"

She slapped me across my face again and this time

my lip cut open. "Olodo (An insult; an uneducated person) say 'I will tell...' say 'I will tell' **LIES**!" she yelled out again.

I got back up on my knees and then I said, "**I WILL TELL**!" Tears streamed down my face.

"*Food!*" she said.

"*I will eat!*" I replied.

"*Book!*" *she* called out.

"*I don't know,*" I replied.

"*Everything in the house!*" she said.

"*I will destroy,*" I replied.

"*Lies!*" she called out.

"*I will tell,*" I replied.

She repeated it several times more before getting up and walking out. I guess I didn't get the normal beating that day because Dad was in town.

This song was my new name for the next several weeks when Mommy Floressa came home after she'd been out. As she made her way up the stairs, she'd call out "Food!" and I'd respond back with "I will eat!" and when she got to the top of the stairs, I was there to greet her, and she'd proceed to ask what I had broken in the house that day, then walked off with a long hiss without waiting to hear a response.

Eight

AGE 24 - 33

"I don't seem to be good enough for him anymore, no matter what I do. I'm a good cook, a good mom, I keep the house clean, I've lost my baby weight, I make sure I look good when we're going out, anytime he's horny I never deny him sex, I allow him to keep his hobbies no matter that I feel it's a waste of money. What haven't I done for this man? Am I not worth a 'Baby, are you ok?' from him?" I cried these words to my older sister Uche who had been my 'go-to-person' in times of marital crisis.

I was in tears while we sat in a corner of the coffee

shop we'd meet up at once a month or so. Uche had gotten married about two years after me, and it felt good to have someone I could call on who could understand my occasional marital struggles. Uche had told me she knew she had married her soul mate. She was always so happy. She never seemed to have any problems in her marriage and I sometimes wondered what was making mine so different.

"Oma! Sounds like he may just be going through some difficulties in his life right now and it may be coming off as you being the problem. Sis, don't feel like you're the problem, because you're clearly not; maybe he just needs someone to listen to him and talk to him about what he may be going through. Have you tried asking him what is wrong?" Uche asked.

I shook my head as I blew my nose "He hasn't even stopped to ask *me* what's wrong with me. Must it always be about him? Every time we have problems, he gets in one of his moods, and I'm always the one who ends up asking him what the matter is and if we can talk about it. And no matter what I tell him that he's done to hurt me, somehow I always end up being the one who apologizes. He never ever says 'I'm sorry' to me anymore. Uche! Am I not worth an 'I'm sorry?' Sometimes one needs to hear it and feel it."

I started to sob again. "Uche, I'm just tired, I'm tired of not being relevant in his life anymore. If this is truly who he is, then he lied to me all this time, pretending to be someone he clearly isn't."

"Stop, Oma!" Uche stopped me. "Stop getting over-excited. I know you're hurting right now, but you can't let your thoughts run wild. Sebastian loves you and everyone knows and sees it. You guys are just going through a hard time right now. All married couples go through them, and you're gonna get through it. I promise. Just keep on doing what you've been doing, talk to him even if he doesn't respond, and remember to keep praying. God has gotten us through a lot as kids and He's not going to stop now. Oma, you've come too long a way to let a man break your spirit now. If Floressa couldn't break our spirits as children, who is Sebastian to try to break it now as an adult?"

I stopped crying. Uche was right. We had grown so strong together as sisters along with Ada and we had gotten through some impossible situations by ourselves. Why was I letting this man break me now? I saw that I had let all of me go and put *everything* I was in this one man, and right then, I was going to stop. "Thanks, Uche, I really appreciate you. You've always been there for me and you're always there to listen to me no matter how redundant it can get. I know you have your own issues to deal with and I'm always bringing my own to you."

Uche quickly shook her head. "No, no, Oma! You never bother me. You're my sister, and I love you and I will always, always be here for you, no matter what I may be going through. Always remember that. Ok?" I nodded and we embraced.

I thought to myself: *I'm not going to stop being a wife to my husband. No; far from it. Rather, I am just going to be there for him and my children, while also being there for myself.* I had set goals and plans for myself in the past, and it was time for me to accomplish them.

I went back to school and I earned my second Bachelor's degree in Business, and put all my time and energy into building my business.

AGE 4 - 13

In 1987, Floressa had Nnamdi, her second son. Ada and Uche were out of the house in boarding school about five hours away from home by road, and Daddy was in the United States as usual. We had one house-girl at the time who Floressa kept very busy with errands, so I remember being very lonely a lot.

It was mid-February and I was playing with my toys in my room and Floressa was in the living room with Christian Jr. and Nnamdi. "Oma!" she called for me.

"Yes, Mommy!" I quickly replied. I ran up to the living room to see what she needed. She was sitting in the living room signing a birthday card for Dad so she could mail it to him in the U.S for his birthday, which was in early March; she wanted to get it to him on time. "Come and sign your name on here for your daddy's birthday."

I started to tremble because I knew Floressa had beaten me and cursed me many times before because my writing and spelling were so bad. I wanted to make sure I wrote my name as perfectly as I could get it. I took the pen she handed me. I saw she had signed Ada's name, Uche's name, and then my name should come next. Gently, I began to write my name, and after I finished writing it, I put a period after it. She then knocked me on the head with a closed fist and then slapped me across my face.

"ARE YOU THE LAST CHILD?" she yelled at me. "Do you think you are the last child? So are Junior and Nnamdi not your father's children, too?" She pushed me away with her forearm as I looked at her with tears in my eyes. *I can't even get this right,* I thought to myself. I stood there in front of her in case she was not done scolding me. I noticed her as she changed the period into a comma, and that's how I learned a period comes when a sentence is over and you use a comma when listing things.

The following year, I was sent off to boarding school with my sisters. We went to John F. Kennedy International School in Warri which, again, was about five hours away from home. It was great! And then Floressa started to travel to the U.S with Dad; Junior and Nnamdi would stay with Floressa's mother and her sister at their home in Maryland Nigeria.

Boarding school was a bitter-sweet experience. It was a breath of fresh air compared to living at home with Floressa. And that's where Ada, Uche and I really became closer because it was such a harsh environment of living in hostels with all girls and girls getting into fights with each other over mostly trivial things, and the dormitory routine was a very strict schedule. We woke up early mornings by 4 a.m. We had to have our bath-buckets filled with water that was fetched from the well the evening before and put under our bunk-beds for bathing the next morning.

Uche and I usually partnered up; she'd quickly get me up. "Oma, get up! Get up! Let's go before the line gets too long."

She'd rush me out of bed and I could still barely keep my eyes open. It was warm in my bed, cold and dark outside and I had to wrestle with getting out of bed. When I'd finally get up, Uche and I would hold opposite ends of this heavy bucket of water and carry it quickly across to the next building which was the bath-house building. We'd hurry in the dark through muddy grass most of the time, due to the girls ahead of us spilling water from their buckets in their haste.

Sometimes Uche and I would be among the first girls taking our baths; other times we'd have to wait for those ahead of us to finish. If we were ever late for one thing, it most often affected the next thing we needed to get done on the schedule.

After our morning baths, we'd put on our blue and

white-striped uniforms that had to be washed and pressed the night before. We then had to go to the designated classrooms which were on the other end of campus that was a good half a mile away from the hostels for study time. We were required to study until the bell for breakfast rang, at which point we'd have to scurry back towards the cafeteria which was next to our dorms to get in line with our plates in hand ready for our meals. Of course, we had only a limited amount of time to eat. When the bell for classes would ring we had to yet again hurry back to the front of the school. It was quite an exercising experience.

All the students, both *day* students (those who didn't live on campus) and boarding school students, were to get in line according to their class and grade, and announcements for the day would be made by the principal. We as a school would have to sing the national anthem, pledge of allegiance and then sing the school song. Then the school prefect and school mother (usually a woman who looks after the girls in the school) would state the hairstyle all the girls were required to have for the week.

And sometimes, if any student had to be disciplined by the staff for any reason, it generally was done in front of the school to set an example to the rest. The disobedient student would be beaten with a cane (usually a long, thick stick) on his/her back or hand; most of the time the girls got it on their hands and boys on their bottoms and back.

After the announcements and disciplines, we'd be sent off to start our classes. After the first set of classes, at noon, the bell for lunch would ring and all the boarding house students would run back towards the cafeteria to have our lunch. After lunch we were required to have our siesta for about an hour before classes resumed. After school for the day, day students went home, the gates were locked, and boarding house students stayed on campus and had some free time before dinner. At 5 p.m. dinner would be served, then we would go back and study in the classrooms for a couple of hours to do our homework assignments and any projects, and then it was bedtime. That was the boarding school schedule we were meant to follow every day; needless to say, not all students followed it.

Ada had come to this boarding school first, and then a year later, Uche came, and then a year after that, I came. So I was at this boarding school for only a year and Ada had known most of the students and teachers there for two years.

Some of the gossip we as new students used to hear

was that Warri was a state in Nigeria well known for witchcraft and many evil things; and some of the students had many stories of experiences 'they had had' over one evil spirit or another. Once, I saw some senior girls (Girls in higher grade levels than I was in), about four of them at the time, surround this little girl who had just been admitted to the school and who couldn't have been older than four or five. They accused her of being a witch and one of the senior girls told the other girls standing there that the night before she had seen a cat outside the dorm, and she picked up a stone and threw the stone at the cat and hit the cat on the head and it ran away towards the little girls' dormitory.

And now this morning, the little girl woke up with a scar on her forehead. They kept questioning her, asking her if she was that cat, and asking her how she got the cut on her forehead? They kept asking her what she was looking for in our dormitory last night. Finally the girl nodded yes, she was the cat. I wondered, *where would the senior girl have gotten a stone to throw at the cat if she were inside the dorm room?* And this poor little girl looked so scared as those girls were taunting her.

But who was I to do anything? I couldn't defend her. I didn't even know her. I kept watching from my bed the chaos that was slowly beginning to grow as other girls started to come closer to see what was going on. Ada came and pulled me away from my bed to go outside and she told me to go wash my uniform and other clothes for tomorrow.

Ada usually tried to keep Uche and me away from any kind of confrontations or 'evil spirit' discussions, which happened often. She made sure we all went to church every Sunday and that we remained prayerful every day.

The gates of the school were only opened on Sundays to allow students to go to church. The proprietor of the school insisted every Christian student go to the Catholic Church, but my sisters and I weren't Catholic and didn't want to go to the Catholic Church as instructed. So while walking to church on Sundays, we'd pull away from the group of students walking towards the Catholic church and go to our non-denominational church, about ten minutes away from the Catholic church. However, we would have to leave our church an hour later, even though the service wasn't over, so we could catch up with the group of other students who had got out of their one-hour Catholic Church service.

Ada, Uche and I spent our days at boarding school following most of the strict schedules, and we tried mostly to keep to ourselves so as to avoid trouble with other girls and avoid gossip, because gossip was rampant, and often led to many fights at the school.

Nine

AGE 4 - 13

It was about 4 p.m. on Friday, the last week of school, and I was walking back towards my hostel from the front of the school after seeing off one of my friends who was a day student. My math teacher, who was maybe in his late-thirties or early forties, short, medium-sized and usually had a firm tone when addressing his students in class, was standing in front of the teacher's dorm not far from the front of the school. He waved for me to come over to join him when he saw me walking. I walked over to him and greeted him "Good afternoon, Mr. Segun."

"Good afternoon, Oma. How are you? he said.

"Fine, thank you, sir." I said.

"Where are you coming from? he asked.

"I just saw my friend Jennifer off, sir. Now I'm going back to my hostel."

He stepped closer to me, and put his arm around my shoulder with a smile on his face. "When are you leaving for home?" he asked.

"Tomorrow, sir," I replied with a bit of confusion in my mind as I wasn't used to male teachers wrapping their arms around me.

"Ok, ok, that's good. Come inside, I have a small present for you to take home, ok? For being one of my best students this year. Come, come."

Best students? I thought to myself. I had never been the top student in any of my classes. We hadn't gotten our report cards yet, so maybe I had done very well this term, and if that was the case, I couldn't wait to tell Mommy Floressa because she promised to kill a cow for me if I ever came first in my class. He walked me into the teacher's building and into his living quarters. In his one-room unit, there was a bed, a small couch, a table with some notebooks and text-books and a chair. He sat me down on his bed.

"You know you've been one of my best students

this year. Right Oma? You are such a fine girl, eh! Oma, Oma," Mr. Segun said. Then he sat next to me and began to caress my thigh. I quickly shifted my thigh away from his hand, hoping he'd go and get the present so I could leave. He then said to me, "Come, let us play," as he wrapped his arm around my shoulder, pulling me closer to him. That was the first time I had ever heard that term "let us play", and in that moment I knew it wasn't the same playing I was used to doing with my friends. Fear suddenly overcame me and I shot up from his bed and said, "Sorry, sir, but I have to go; my sisters are waiting for me."

"But come now, I haven't given you the present yet." He began to reach into his pocket as if to bring out some money to give me, but I was so taken aback with the whole situation that I sprinted out of his room before he got upset at me for not "playing" with him. I didn't tell Ada because she would have been angry at me for still being in front of the school by that time.

I stayed at JFK boarding school only one year before my sisters and I were transferred to a boarding school closer to home in Lagos. At age eleven, I started at A-Z International School in Ikeja along with my sisters. It was a prestigious, newly opened private school at the time. We spent the rest of our schooling years there before being sent to the U.S. My sisters and I had gotten used to depending on each other after our experiences at JFK without our parents there, so now, at a new boarding school, we became more like best friends and had gotten used to relying on each other. I remember when Uche was finishing J.S.S. 3 (Junior Secondary School 3; middle school) and had taken an entrance exam to get into S.S. 1 (Senior Secondary 1; high school). After the exam she got to be out of school for about a month. I was going to miss her terribly; I was closer to her than Ada because she was my immediate older sister and she was closer to my age than Ada. During the first week of school, I had already begun missing her, so when I arrived at school, I wrote Uche a letter to tell her how everything was going so far.

A-Z International School

P.O. Box 5006

M.M Airport

Ikeja, Lagos

25th of Oct 1990

Dear Sister Uche,

How are you? I hope you are feeling fine? How is home? I hope it is also alright? Well I wanted to write how I feel sad and lonely here I feel so emtey. Uche *if you* resived this letter before 25th of oct it is 16 of oct not 25th I am writing on the same day we came I can't just stay like this without talking or writing to you Uche please don't forget to come and visit us.

Uche if Daddy or Mummy phones tell them that papa Chisom is coming to America on the 20th of November that we are finishing our exam on 22nd of November that we are starting on Monday the next Monday. I was studing before I wrote this letter. Tell daddy to tell papa Chisom to come and pick me so I can go with him. Or I can come on the 30th of November that please I am begging him and he should write to me too.

Uche I am very sorry I have to end my letter here I love and miss you very much.

Give me a smile J
Lots & lots of love

Oma
Reply soon
P.S: Uche Guess what. Ada has started her menstruation her period. Is it not wonderfull?

Clearly, my spelling, finished thoughts and punctuation needed a bit of work at that time!

Ada, Uche and I spent a lot of our time in boarding school writing letters to each other and, of course, to Dad, who was mostly in the U.S during that time. We missed him terribly and often tried to say almost anything to get him to either come visit us, or send for us to come to the U.S.

In 1990, we were home on vacation from school. That was the year we had first contact from our mother Denise. It was around 7 p.m. in the evening and my Aunty Nkechi had arrived in Nigeria visiting from the United States. She came in straight from the airport to Uncle BM's house which was right next door to our house. When she arrived, we ran downstairs from our house to greet her and to see if Dad (who was in the U.S. at the time) had sent anything with her for us. But our biggest surprise was that, she had gifts not only from Dad, but also from someone we had never expected to hear from.

"From your Mommy Denise," Aunty Nkechi said to us as she handed us a black plastic bag. In the bag were letters, soaps with scents we'd never smelled before that smelled like heaven, beautiful letter stationeries, stickers of all colors, shapes and sizes and a cassette tape. "Do you guys remember her?" Aunty asked.

Did we? Was she kidding? We had a huge framed

picture of her holding Ada as a baby with Dad behind her in our house, plus we had albums and albums of her and Dad together in one of his traveling trunks that we often went through whenever Mommy Floressa wasn't around. She was the most beautiful woman in the world to us and now we were getting letters from her?

"Yes Aunty!" we replied her in harmony. "We remember her."

"Ok," replied Aunty Nkechi, "she asked me to make sure you girls got this package from her, ok?" She handed it to Ada.

Boy! That was the most beautiful-looking, wonderful-smelling package my sisters and I had ever gotten in our entire lives, and we couldn't get upstairs to our house fast enough to read our letters. We went into our empty house (as both Dad and Mommy Floressa were in America). We had no house-help living with us and we usually went upstairs with our cousins to play and hang out most of the day, but this time, we needed some privacy.

We dashed into our room and closed our bedroom door behind us. It was starting to get dark outside, so we turned our bedroom light on and drew our curtains closed to ensure further privacy (as if anyone could see us, being on the topmost floor of the building). Ada opened the letter and slowly began to read it out loud. It was the very first time we were hearing from our birth mother and it felt like it wasn't really happening. Ada read the letter so slowly, and I could tell we were all feeling the same way…not wanting the moment to end, not wanting the letter to end. -

Alpine Road
Berkeley CA.

My dearest daughters,

I truly hope this letter finds you this time. I ran into your Aunty Nkechi while shopping and she told me she was planning a trip to Nigeria soon. I told her I'd like to send you girls a few things and she promised she would get it to you girls. I want to make sure this time I send you as much as I can, and see if you girls get it.

I need you girls to know that I have tried writing you guys all these years and I have given your father several letters for you over the years, but I suspect you never received them because I never got a reply. There is so much I want to tell you girls, how much Mommy loves you, how much I miss you, I want to tell you about what happened between your father and I. But Mommy hopes that someday, I'll be able to see you girls and we can talk all about that. I have included in this parcel a tape with some of your cousins, aunties, uncles, and your little brother Jean-Pierre. They all miss you girls so much as well, I thought you girls would love to know who they are, too. We all pray for you girls every single day, we pray that we get to see you all soon, we pray that you all are doing well in school, that you're safe and happy. I have included my address at the top of this letter and also included Grandma's address on the tape as well, because Grandma has been at her address for a very long time. Ada, Mommy loves you! Uche, Mommy loves you! And Oma, my baby, Mommy loves you! Please write soon.

Always
Your mommy
Denise

After Ada finished the letter, we then played the cassette tape...*HER VOICE!* She had the most softly spoken voice we had ever heard. She sounded like an angel to us. She said all the things we wanted and needed to hear from a mom. I looked at Uche and Ada as we listened to the tape and saw that we all had to be feeling the exact same way. Was this really happening? After Mom spoke, she introduced our little brother to us on the tape; she told us we had a little brother and his name was Jean-Pierre (JP). She asked JP to tell us about himself. JP told us his name, his birth date and his age. He even told us a story about a boy who lost his favorite toy. He sounded so cute and so American and I was tickled by his story. After his story, Mom came back on and said she'd like to share with us her favorite song, and then she began singing:

> "*He's precious to meeee, so precious to me,*
> *what a wonderful savior is heeeee,*
> *the longer I serve him, more truly I find*
> *that Jesus is precious to meeee!*
> *Oh yes he's precious to me, so precious to me.*
> *What a wonderful savior is heeee*
> *the longer I serve him more truly I find,*
> *that Jesus is precious to meeee!*"

Then she said, "Jean-Pierre's gonna sing with me now," and they both began to sing the song again and at that point I started tearing up because I had become so overwhelmed with an overflow of emotion, I couldn't hold it in any longer. I was hearing my mother's voice for the first time, I had a little brother I had never met, and I was hearing his voice for the first time; they believed in God the same way I had been raised to believe in God and they were both singing to us so beautifully.

One the rest of the tape we were introduced to our other family members: Grandma, uncles, aunties, and cousins. We had no idea we were even ever thought about by Mommy Denise, but a whole family of people who knew us, missed us, prayed for us, and loved us was out there? In my mind that was nothing short of a miracle because I was told countless times from Mommy Floressa, as she was beating me, that I was so useless, that even our own mother didn't want us. She said we had written our own mother letters and she had sent the letters back unopened because she didn't want anything to do with us.

Mommy Denise left her address on the tape recording and asked us to write her anytime as often as we'd like and she would always reply. As if she knew we had not been able to reach her all that time.

Ada, Uche and I spent the rest of that evening listening to the tape over and over again. We stopped long enough to take our baths with the soap she sent us that we absolutely loved the smell of. Our baths from that day onwards were so awesome because the house smelled of heaven and helped remind us of our Mom every day, until we used up the soaps.

We spent most of the following days writing letters to her and other family members we had just been introduced to. Ada told us this had to remain a secret from Dad and Mommy Floressa and I didn't understand at the time why, but I definitely listened to sister Ada and I never told Dad that we were writing Mom. The following year, June 1991, when I was age twelve, Dad sent for me and Uche in the United States.

Ten

AGE 24 - 33

Sebastian had been spending more and more time out. He seemed to be having more 'business meetings' and out-of-town organization functions, which I had usually attended with him, but seeing how we hadn't been on the best of terms the past few months it didn't matter. Plus, I wasn't exactly feeling left out for not being invited because I was now focused on me.

I used the time he was away to get in shape, grow my business, attend the kids' extra-curricular sports activities, and go on outings with friends and lunch/dinner with my siblings. I especially reignited some long-term friendships that had dwindled away since I had gotten married. It felt like a newfound freedom I had lost for years and for some reason, I didn't care that Sebastian was gone nor did I wonder what he may have been doing. I noticed, but didn't care to know why he suddenly changed his cell phone password, bank accounts and email passwords he had once given me access to. I didn't care so much that he suddenly had to leave the room to take a call where he had comfortably talked in front of me in the past. I just....didn't care anymore. Matter of fact, it allowed me my 'me' time to go out and to talk with *my* friends freely on the phone.

"Hummm...so you're going out again today? Another party?" Victor asked me over our now regular telephone calls. Victor and I had gone to high school together, and we had been good friends for over ten years. Victor was a tall and handsome Mexican with a smile that could make any woman fall to her knees. He had a very friendly and approachable personality, and when I first met him at school we hit it off right away, but only as friends, and it pretty much had stayed that way ever since. We had attended each other's college graduations, weddings, children's birthday parties with our spouses and so on. He ended up marrying this 'supermodel-esque' girl who also happened to be down-to-earth, and intelligent; she was quite a catch. I had to give it up to him when he got married, jokingly asking him how he managed to get her to say yes. But I knew he was a good guy and any woman would be lucky to have him.

"Oh, yes. You know I can't stay cooped up in this house too long. All work and no play make-woman-very-sad-woman," I replied jokingly in a cave-woman tone. Victor had always been a good listener, and he was easy to talk to. He had no judgments about my flaws, yet he knew how to tell me when I was wrong. That didn't always feel good to hear, but it definitely helped me 'shape-up' when I needed to.

"Ok, so what are you wearing tonight?" Victor asked. "I know you had to go shopping now that you've lost all your baby weight."

"Well, I got this really nice black dress, but what makes it cool is that it has these leather linings in the waist area which allows it to hug my body and show my curves," I replied as I stood in front of the mirror getting dressed.

"Send me a picture so I can see."

I got my cell phone from on top of the bed and took a full-body picture in the mirror and hit send. "Did you get it? Whatcha think?"

Victor was silent for a minute or so "Hmmm!! Girl, don't hurt nobody now!"

I guess that means I look, hot, I said to myself, loving the response he gave. It suddenly dawned on me that it had been years since any sort of compliment has been said to me telling me that I was beautiful; and right then, it felt good hearing it.

As time went on, Victor and I spent more and more time talking on the phone, and confiding in each other. We had always stayed in touch, and spoken with each other maybe once every three or four months. But, our talks had been increasing slowly from monthly, to weekly, and now, we spoke to each other at least two or three times a day. Our talks were mostly about trivial, casual things. Like, I'd see something funny on TV and call him to turn to the channel and we'd have a laugh together. He could be having a bad day at work, and he'd call me to vent about it.

I then started confiding in him about my marriage issues, initially to get a 'guy's point of view' and he'd comfort me when I started crying. He advised me on what to try differently with Sebastian, or told me what Sebastian was doing wrong and how to handle it. He also assured me that there was nothing I was doing wrong to deserve the way I was being treated. He'd tell me how beautiful I was; when I told him how I hadn't heard that in so long.

He'd tell me how men would be lining up around the block waiting for me to be single again and jokingly added that he'd be standing in front of that line. He had constantly asked my permission to confront Sebastian about his behavior towards me, assuring me that we were all friends and he should be able to talk to Sebastian on my behalf. But I'd tell him Sebastian might not see it Victor's way because Sebastian might feel Victor was taking my side because Victor and I were friends first. Victor and my talks were so easy, comfortable, familiar, and innocent (with subtle hints of flirtation) and I enjoyed them.

AGE 4 - 13

It was early 1991. Uche and I were sent for first, as Ada was in her last year of high school and Dad wanted her to finish high school before coming to the U.S. I was so happy to be in the United States. I had begged and pleaded with Dad for so many years to bring us back out to the U.S. and he always replied, "Soon." Now we were finally here! Dad and Mommy Floressa had been living in a two-bedroom one-bath apartment in San Pablo, California, and, though the apartment was much smaller than our home in Nigeria, I wouldn't have traded it for a moment. I was not only happy to be in the U.S., but was ecstatic to be with Dad again, and this time it seemed to be for good. On our first weekend in the U.S., Dad took Uche and me around the city to see the lights, buildings and stores. He took us clothes and shoes shopping and I was just elated and bursting with glee over being with my Dad. Mommy Floressa was at work on that day, so it was nice having alone time with just me, Uche and Dad.

One Wednesday morning while Dad was at work, there was a knock at our front door. Floressa went from the kitchen where she was cooking, opened the door, and there were two police officers standing there.

"Good morning, ma'am! We're looking for a Mr. Christian Banufo?"

Floressa looked stunned and confused. "He's not home right now, but I'm his wife. Can I help you?"

One of the officers looked into the apartment and noticed me and Uche sitting in the living room.

"Ma'am, may we come in? This is in regard to the girls."

Floressa looked back at us with a bit of confusion and a hint of fear, not sure if we may have called the cops on her without her knowledge. She stepped back and let the police officers in.

"Ma'am, are you familiar with a Denise Brough?"

Floressa's face showed more signs of confusion as she responded to the officers with even more fear in her voice…"Yes, sir, I do. She is their biological mother," she said, and then quickly added, "but I've been the one raising these girls since they were babies!"

"Ma'am, we've been ordered to take these girls with us to the police station right now. You may want to call your husband to inform him to come to the station as soon as possible as we have a warrant out for his arrest for the kidnapping of these girls over ten years ago."

"WHAAAAT?!!!!" Floressa screamed and started

to jump in place, she fell to her knees and began to beg the police officers. "PLEASE, PLEASE, DON'T TAKE MY KIDS! PLEASE, OFFICERS, I LOVE THEM SO MUCH! WHAT AM I SUPPOSED TO DO?"

This was shocking to me. As I witnessed her behavior, I, for one, thought she would have been excited to see us go. I was sure this was all an act for the officers and for us so if anyone were to ask what happened she could say she was begging and pleading for us. There was nothing in the history I had spent with Floressa that equated with her behavior at that moment.

I was jumping for joy inside because I couldn't wait for the officers to get me out of that house and away from her. It hadn't even hit me at all why we were being taken away; all I knew was that I was being saved from Floressa. We were allowed to put on some decent clothes. I wore blue jeans and a simple white shirt with a printed logo of a cartoon character, and a dark blue, puffy jacket. Uche put on a long skirt and knitted sweater, and we walked out of the house with the police officers with visibly sad faces on, but I was bursting for joy inside.

We arrived at the police station in San Pablo some ten minutes later and were taken into a back room with both uniformed and un-uniformed staff. A woman sat with us briefly and asked us some questions. She was an older white woman in what seemed to be her mid to late-forties; she had dark blonde hair and very little make-up on. I later found out she was what is called a social worker, but to me, a twelve-year old girl who just arrived some two months before from Nigeria, she was just a nice woman asking about me and my sister.

"Do you girls know where you are?" she asked in the softest voice I'd heard since I'd been in the country.

"Yes!" Uche replied.

I sat there silently, not knowing where I was, and was shocked that Uche did. Did I miss something? How come Uche knew what was going on and I didn't? But Uche had always been observant of things. She always knew what to say, how to say it and had always been smart.

"Where are you?" the nice lady asked.

"We are at the police station," Uche replied.

"Do you know why you are here?"

"Because my mom wants us back."

What? I thought to myself. Floressa wants us back? No, no, no, no! I'm not going back to that woman. I said to the lady, "Please don't take us back there. I don't want to go back home!" She held my shoulder with both hands.

"No, Oma, we're not taking you back home. Your mom is coming to get you right now. Do you know who your mom is?"

I turned and looked at Uche, expressing a bit of confusion because I had been beaten on so many occasions by Floressa telling me she was my mom and I should never call her step-mother or tell people she was my step-mom. So the only woman I knew as a mom was Floressa. And as if Uche knew what I was thinking in that moment, she said to me,

"Denise. She's talking about Mommy Denise."

Oh my God! I thought to myself, *I'm going to get to see my birth mom today?* I stood there shocked, excited, nervous, and scared all at once. After she was done with her questions, the nice lady finally left Uche and me in an office. Uche and I sat silently in our seats, nervously waiting for our mom. I heard some voices outside the office, not right outside the door but several feet away, so I anxiously cracked open the door to see if I could get a glimpse of her before she came in. But I couldn't see her, or could I? I wasn't even sure what she looked like. All I knew of her was from pictures we had back home in Nigeria, and those were from when Ada was still a baby. Besides, all I could see at that point looking through the cracked door were the backs of people standing and huddling in a corner. I slowly shut the door and looked over at Uche. Uche still sat silently with a sad look on her face.

"I think she's here!" I said to her, thinking maybe she was sad because Mommy Denise wasn't here yet. But Uche still sat in the chair with her head hanging low. I soon copied her demeanor as maybe that was the right way to behave right now; I wasn't supposed to be 'happy' about our situation, and Uche always knew how to behave and did everything right and rarely ever got into trouble. I didn't want to get into any trouble with Denise for misbehaving, so I sat down silently in my chair, hung my head down and expressed sadness.

Denise soon walked in the door. She came in with tears already in her eyes, and she looked at Uche and me for maybe all of three seconds and quickly grabbed us both from our seats into her long, wide arms, squeezed us both tightly into her bosom and began to sob. I had never been held so tightly before in my life, but it felt like a good kind of tight. We all three soon started sobbing uncontrollably in each other's arms as we stood there for what felt like ages. She gently pulled us back away from her and took a look at us, and we at her. She was over six feet tall and had squinty eyes, lighter skin than ours, huge breasts like Floressa, a beautiful face, and long fingers. She wore a long denim dress and white tennis shoes and held a brown purse. She sat down and had us sit right next to her and had a smile on her face as big as it could possibly get.

"My babies! My beautiful, beautiful babies!" she said as tears continued to fall from her eyes with a smile on her face. "Do you know who I am?" she asked us,

"Yes!" Uche answered. "You're Mommy Denise."

"Yes, that's right! I'm Mommy Denise," she repeated as if she knew we had to differentiate the m*ommies* in our lives.

"Are you going to take us home with you?" I asked as she wiped the tears from my face.

"Yes, love! You girls are coming with me. Are you hungry?"

"Yes!" I replied as fast as she had asked the question, and almost as soon covered my mouth, afraid that I had answered so quickly because such a reaction to food with Floressa would have irritated her. But Mommy Denise didn't appear irritated by my quick response. In fact, she seemed happy that I said yes I was hungry. As soon as I realized that, my heartbeat slowed down and I knew I was in safer hands and I could eat without feeling guilty.

"We're gonna go to church first because everyone is

waiting for you girls at church. Then we'll all eat together at church. And Jean-Pierre's at church, too! Do you girls remember Jean-Pierre?"

"Yes, Mommy!" I replied. "He's my little brother. Does he know we're coming?" I asked with excitement.

"Yes, sweetheart! Everyone knows I'm bringing you girls with me."

Now I didn't fully know what she meant by *everyone* in that moment; as far as I knew, everyone meant the family members we listened to on the tape she sent us last year.

We arrived at her church (*Assembly of God*) in Berkeley about a half-hour later and we walked in holding our mom's hands. Everyone in the church turned around what seemed like one at a time, looking back at us. Then we began hearing whispering within the congregation, then soft sounds of "Praise the Lord!", "Praise the Lord", and the then soft cries of strangers I'd never met before crying uncontrollably as they saw us walk in. We stood at the doors of the entrance for a while as the whole church finally began to sing praises and weeping. As we walked down the aisle towards the front, people came out from their seats in no particular order and came up to us hugging, crying, weeping, their arms lifted up in the air shouting out,

"Praise God!!" and each of them saying to us, "We have been praying for you girls for so long, hallelujah!"

I hadn't experienced such a show of love and emotion from anyone before, let alone strangers who didn't know me. I started looking around the whole church, looking for my brother JP to see if I could find him; there were so many people there and all were crying and holding me, but I kept trying to find JP, and finally I did. I spotted him in the middle of one of the aisles and I saw him trying to get through people to get to us, but the congregation unknowingly overwhelmed his efforts.

Finally someone took notice and let me get through and I finally got to JP. I embraced him as hard as Mommy Denise had embraced me just hours before. I knew him immediately because he looked just like me; this was my baby brother and I loved him already. That evening was nothing short of a miracle in my sister Uche's and my lives, and I felt love.

Ada was sent for not too long after that day, but her coming here to the United States was not on a very happy note for her.

Eleven

AGE 4 - 13

It was heavenly getting to live with Mom. She cooked such wonderful-smelling and tasting foods I hadn't had before, like macaroni and cheese, pancakes from scratch, greens (that took some getting used to), spaghetti with meatballs, lasagna, just so many different delicious foods. She taught us how to eat spaghetti with a spoon and fork so it could be eaten neatly; now that was cool. She showed us how to put napkins on our laps when eating to prevent food from staining our clothes.

The early days and weeks were sublime and I was happy to be getting to know her and my brother, all their ways, beliefs, habits and so forth. But unfortunately, the bliss didn't last very long. Mommy Denise's way of living was a lot different than the way we were used to living, both in Nigeria and here in America. There certainly weren't any more random beatings for one thing or another, that was for sure, but Mommy Denise was a different kind of different. She didn't believe in watching television, and we were used to watching TV every day. She went to church every other day, and we were used to going only on Sundays. We weren't allowed to listen to music on the radio, and we were used to listening to and dancing to music from Dad's records. We had to wear stockings when we wore dresses to church, and that was just torture for a twelve-year old. We were used to saying "I want to shit" when we needed to go number two, but JP always complained to Mom that we were cursing and that was just confusing; how was 'shit' a bad word? Quite strange.

We were also not allowed to call or speak to our father; that was the most difficult part for me. Dad was my warm blanket, my best friend; he was fun to be around, took us to fun places, bought us nice things, let us speak our minds and was simply the best dad to me…when he was around.

I mentioned earlier how Ada's arrival to the United

States wasn't a happy one for her. Well, unbeknownst to me at my young, naïve and immature age, Dad had been arrested and charged with kidnapping Ada, Uche and me over ten years ago, because Mom had won custody of us when they got a divorce. And on his first visitation day with us girls, Dad took us to Nigeria and never brought us back. That was why he and some of his family hadn't let us have contact with her all that time.

Dad was told bail would be set for him only after he arranged for Ada to be brought out here. My dad's family immediately began the process and Ada soon joined us at Mom's house. I was quite shocked to see her so soon because she was supposed to finish high school before coming, but again, being blinded by my joy to see her, I didn't realize she wasn't very happy. Ada apparently had gotten a lot of heat from Dad's family members for writing to Mommy Denise telling her Uche and I were now in the U.S. That's how Mommy Denise knew where to send the cops to come get us. Ada was just a daughter, fourteen-years old at the time, writing to her mother, letting her mom know her sisters were in the U.S now and could go see them if she wanted to. Ada had no knowledge of what had occurred ten years prior, and even if she had, I doubt she could have known the consequences of what might happen to Dad.

So Ada was chastised, beaten, insulted and consequently blamed by uncles and aunts for having her father arrested and Uche and Oma taken away from their home. Ada didn't get to finish high school in Nigeria with her friends, and she didn't come to the U.S into the loving arms of Mom, Dad or sisters; she was interviewed by lawyers and then released to the mother she had never met. My sister was sad and it broke my heart. After the court proceedings, Mom dropped the charges on Dad on the condition that she got sole and physical custody of us, our passports were to be held by the courts until we were eighteen so neither parent was allowed to take us out of the country again, and that he stay away from all of us, including JP.

Our stay with Mommy Denise only lasted for about four months. Mommy Denise had gone from having one child, Jean-Pierre for the past eight years with a single-family income and a simple lifestyle, to having three additional children - one pre-teen, and two teenage girls - added to her home overnight. We had been raised with a different culture, and different way of life, a different way of eating, thinking, talking, and interacting. She still had the same income as she did before we came, with no financial support and the same small, two-bedroom apartment. In the end, after we had

139

this major change in our lives and this was supposed to be our new way of living, my sisters and I just weren't happy. We missed our father. I think it may have just been me who didn't know what had transpired with Dad, so all I wanted to do was go home to him.

It was a Saturday morning in late-July 1991. Mommy Denise had gone to work and Ada, Uche and I woke up as usual in our bedroom and said our prayers individually on our knees. My prayers were pretty quick. I'd thank God for life, ask for forgiveness for my sins and ask for blessings for me and my family. Done! I never understood why it took my sisters so long to pray. I had other things to do - like play. So I left them in the room and went out to the living room where JP slept, to bother him. About an hour later, Ada and Uche came out of the bedroom fully dressed with their shoes and jackets on and said to me,

"Oma, stay here with JP. We'll be back soon. And don't open the door for anyone."

"Where are you guys going?" JP asked as though he were in charge, because he knew we weren't supposed to be leaving the house while Mom wasn't home.

"None of your business," Uche blurted out to him as she and Ada walked out the door.

"I'm gonna tell Mom!" JP shouted after them

outside the apartment door as they walked down the staircase.

"Jean-Pierre, come back in here!" I said to him, attempting to sound authoritative as an older sister; I was still trying to get the hang of being an older sister to a walking, talking brother. My half-brothers were still very young and were in Nigeria, so I never got to play the big sister role with them.

"They're not supposed to be going out by themselves!!" JP shouted back at me. "I'm calling Mom at work to tell her!"

"Stop it, Jean-Pierre! And go and sit down now!" I grabbed him and pulled him to the couch. "They said they are coming right back. Why do you want to disturb Mom at work? Leave them alone."

JP had always tried to be the boss in the house and sometimes it was so irritating. So one couldn't even go downstairs from the apartment without having to tell Mom? Na wa oh! (*A sarcastic "wow"*) I wasn't sure where Ada and Uche were going, and it was unusual for them to actually leave the house, but I dared not ask them. I was raised not to question my elders and, having just arrived from Nigeria just five months ago, that was still very much embedded in me.

By the time Mom got home around three o'clock

Ada and Uche weren't back yet but Mom didn't look surprised that they weren't home. In fact, she looked pretty upset. She had Grandma come over to stay with JP and me, and she went back out without saying anything to me or JP. Mom came back a couple of hours later with Ada and Uche and Ada was arguing with her. HARD! I had *never* seen my sister Ada talk to any adult like that before; it was such a foreign sight.

"Why won't you let us stay with our father!? What kind of life is this? We can't even do anything!" Ada shouted at Mommy Denise.

"You disobeyed me!! You took your sister out of this house, went to your father's house even after I told you girls not to!! You are always telling your sisters not to listen to me, you are being very disrespectful and ungrateful!!" Mommy Denise was just as furious with Ada and was yelling right back at her, but that didn't seem to deter Ada.

They went at it with each other while Uche, Jean-Pierre, Grandma and I watched in silence. Ada soon stormed into the bedroom she shared with Uche and me and slammed the door, and Denise did the same to her bedroom and slammed her door. I think we had Top Ramen for dinner that night as neither Ada nor Mommy Denise came out of their rooms the rest of the evening.

It was almost midnight that same night when Mommy Denise woke me and my sisters up. "Get up and put your jackets and shoes on now!" She said firmly while turning our bedroom light on.

I was dazed from being woken up suddenly and being rushed to get dressed. I then noticed that no one was asking where we were going so late. Ada must have still been mad at Mom and Uche must have been her usual quiet self, and I wasn't going to ask any questions because I could feel the tension in the air. We left our pajamas on, put on our coats and house slippers, and took nothing else as Mom hadn't asked us to bring anything else. Jean-Pierre was asleep in the living room with Grandma as we walked through the living room to the front door. We got in the car and Mom started driving. *Where are we going now in the middle of the night?* I thought to myself, feeling extremely sleepy and cold. Mommy Denise didn't utter a word while she drove.

We drove in silence at a fast but steady speed from Berkeley to San Pablo Richmond. She pulled up in front of Dad's apartment, turned around from the driver's seat, and faced us girls sitting in the back seat. "GET OUT! And take those jackets off and leave them in the car!"

What is going on? I thought to myself. This was Dad's apartment; did he know we were coming this late? Did he ask her to bring us? Is she coming in with us?

"GET OUT, YOU UNGRATEFUL BRATS!" she shouted at us as we slowly began to remove our coats. Ada opened the car door and we all stepped out onto the curb. Denise sped away as fast as the car door was closed. She left without even waiting to see if we got into the apartment ok. We walked up the stairs to Dad's apartment unit, knocked on the door several times, as at this point it was late, about 1 a.m. in the morning. Dad came to open to door and had a look of utter shock on his face.

"What are you girls doing here? Where is your mom? How did you guys get here?" he asked, sounding confused, and he appeared to be in a panic.

"Mommy Denise dropped us off here just now," Ada said to Dad.

Dad had us come into the living room and told us to sit on the couch and wait a minute. He said he needed to go get dressed. *Now what?* I thought to myself. *When are we going to get back to bed? It's cold and I'm tired.*

Dad came out of his bedroom moments later fully dressed and said to us, "Let's go!"

"Where are we going?" Uche asked.

"I have to take you girls to the police station and tell them what happened. I'm not supposed to have you girls; I could be arrested again."

Again? I again thought. *When was he ever arrested?* At that time, I hadn't heard about the whole situation that had transpired, so I was thoroughly confused and very sleepy and tired.

We arrived at the police station about ten minutes later. While we were driving to the police station, Dad asked us what had happened, and Ada told Dad about the argument she had had with Mommy Denise just hours before and she believed that may have been what caused her to kick us out. Dad gave his report at the police station asking, the cop at the counter what to do with us as there were court documents against him at that time warning him to stay away from us and that Denise was the one who dropped us off in the middle of the night.

"Do you have any problem keeping your girls?" the police officer asked my father.

"Of course not. They're my children. I'm just here making a report that she was the one who dropped them off at my house and I don't want to be arrested!" my father said in a panicked voice, making sure the police officer was clear about his report.

"Sir, as long as she dropped them off and you have no problem keeping them, you should be ok. You've made your report, and we'll file it," the officer reassured my father. "Just be sure to follow up with your lawyer as soon as you can."

"Ok, thank you!" my dad said to the officer. "Let's go, girls."

We drove back home and I was sitting in the middle of the long coach seat next to Dad in his white with blue striped two-door pick-up with a covered bed. Uche was next to me and Ada was by the passenger side window. I laid my head on Dad's shoulder and I could sense him glance over at me occasionally, most likely admiring and smiling as he often used to do whenever he got back from his long trips. I was finally back home with my Daddy and was Daddy's little girl again.

Twelve

AGE 24 - 33

"Who the hell is Nika! And why have you been calling each other for the past eight months?" It was 9 p.m. at night and Sebastian and I were having yet another fight about his late-night phone calls. Except this time there was finally a name to who had been on the other end of the phone.

"She's nobody, honey. She's just a new employee at my job, and we've been going over work stuff," Sebastian replied, attempting to convince me otherwise of what I was then certain of.

"Sebastian, look at this phone bill." I threw the pages

of that month's cell-phone bill at him and he let them to fall to the floor. "This bill prompted me to go as far back in history as it will allow me, and that is only up to eight months. So, every day for the past eight months you have been calling this same number? And not just during regular hours, but at 1 a.m., 4:25 a.m, and all odd hours!! Tell me, Sebastian, with a straight face that you have been discussing 'work stuff' during those hours?!! And LOOK!" I picked up another page from the previous month's cell-phone bill and pointed to it. "The phone calls seem to have stopped for one full week, which happens to be the same one week you were on one of your out-of-town 'work conferences' in Pasadena!!"

Sebastian took the bill from me, seeming to read it to validate my accusation. "Honey, I swear to you, you are reading more into this than what these bills show. You know I wouldn't do this to you," Sebastian continued to try to reassure me.

"Sebastian." I lowered my voice "Who is she?"

"I swear, it's not what you think, Oma," Sebastian softly replied.

I brought my cell-phone out from the pocket of the robe I had on, and began scrolling through the past dialed numbers. I hadn't yet mentioned to Sebastian that I had already spoken with his 'Nika' earlier on that day and she had told me she worked at his office, but only briefly as she worked through a job-registry. She told me he had invited her out for drinks after her last day of work which was almost a year ago and that Sebastian told her he was recently divorced and wasn't looking for a committed relationship but just needed a friend, which they were initially, but they became intimate weeks later. She said she knew about me, but all this time assumed I was an ex not willing to move on with my life and accept the divorce. She then told me she had come to fall in love with Sebastian and that *her* heart was broken because she couldn't believe that we were still married and not going through a divorce. I had asked her if they ever protected themselves when they were intimate, and she told me they had never used protection and she could never get pregnant because she had a hysterectomy several years ago after some medical complications, as if that would have been the only reason I'd ask. She had immensely apologized to me for any hurt she may have caused, stating that she ended her three-year marriage from a husband who had been physically abusive to her, and didn't want to be the cause of a marriage being broken apart.

I dialed Nika's phone and put it on speaker. "Hello?" Nika answered.

"Hello, Nika, this is Oma calling. I have you on speaker and Sebastian is here. There was something you wanted to say to him?"

"Oh, hello, Oma. Yes there is. Sebastian? Are you there?" Nika asked, but Sebastian refused to answer. "Well, if you can hear me..."

Sebastian quickly grabbed the cell-phone out of my hand and threw it against the wall before Nika could say anything. There was a long silence between us. I couldn't stand to look at him anymore; his behavior and lack of dignity sickened me. I quickly walked out of the room before I started to cry.

"Oma!" Sebastian attempted to stop me, but I kept walking, and he didn't come after me. That man did NOT deserve to see me cry. I didn't want him to mistake my tears for an invitation to console me. Those tears were only to allow me to get out the heartache I was feeling and the shift that had been imminent in our marriage. I knew something was going to change, but I didn't know what that change would be in that moment.

AGE 4 - 13

A few months after the experience with Mommy Denise, my sisters and I were starting to settle in. We were registered at school and back to our usual routine, but we still felt very new in the U.S. and its culture. Unfortunately, Floressa hadn't changed much, but no surprise there. The beatings were starting to get tiring, but I had no idea how to make them stop.

I remember coming back home from school one day and Mommy Floressa and Dad were still at work and Ada and Uche hadn't returned from school yet. I sat in the living room hoping and wishing my sisters would come back home before Mommy Floressa. I was deathly afraid of being alone with her. Suddenly, a desperate feeling came over me. I wanted my Dad to suspect Floressa of cheating; that way, he'd leave her, and the idea that came to me felt brilliant. I was going to be 'attacked' by the jealous boyfriend and be asked to give Floressa a warning to leave her husband for him. I began tearing up the house, I broke plates and glasses in the kitchen, I pulled the covers off the beds and ripped them, I pulled the picture of Dad and Floressa off the wall in the living room, smashed it and scratched

Floressa's face off the picture. Then I picked up the phone and called Dad at work.

"Daddy…Daddy, a man just came in the house and attacked me!" I wailed.

"WHAT? WHO?" Dad shouted in a panic on the other end.

"I don't know him. He was a black man and he told me to tell Mommy to stay away from you!" I cried.

"Where is he now? Has he left?"

"Yes, he ran away. Daddy can you come home, please," I cried.

"I'm coming, I 'm coming right now. I'm going to call the police. Just stay there and don't open the door for anyone, ok? Are your sisters back yet?"

"No, Daddy, they're not."

"Ok, just stay there. I'll be there soon."

The cops got to apartment before Dad got home; they asked me what happened, and I told them the same story, except this time I claimed the man was a white man.

"How did he get in?" one of the Caucasian officers asked.

"I think he came in through my bedroom window. I was in the living room watching TV so I didn't hear him come in," I replied.

The officers went to my bedroom, opened the window and looked out and assessed the scene. "These bushes look undisturbed. No one came in this way," one of the officers said to the other as I looked on.

Dad and Floressa arrived at the same time. The officers spoke with them both outside the apartment. I didn't hear the conversation, but by the looks of it, I was going to be in big trouble. Floressa was slowly slapping her hands together (a motion of disbelief one portrays in the Nigerian culture), and Dad was shaking his head. My father shook the officers' hands and they got in their patrol car and left. Dad and Floressa came up the stairs into the apartment and I stood in the living room with my head hanging low.

"So this is what I brought you to America to come and start doing, Oma?!" Dad scolded. "Oma? What is the matter with you? Why did you do this? When you called me, you told me it was a black man, then when the police came, you told them it was a white man. Are you crazy?" he asked.

I stood in silence, afraid to utter a word. Floressa sat back on the couch without saying anything, looking on as Dad scolded me.

"You're going to clean up every inch of this house! Silly girl…just look at all this mess! C'mon, go and get a broom and start cleaning, and don't try this rubbish again! Do you hear me?!" Dad shouted.

"Yes, Daddy," I softly replied as I went into the kitchen to get the broom.

Dad and Floressa went into their bedroom and Ada and Uche met me cleaning up. Ada asked me what had happened, but I didn't answer her. I just started crying again because I was afraid of what Floressa was going to do to me when Dad was gone. Ada and Uche dropped their backpacks in our bedroom, came out and helped me clean up. When we were all in bed, I then told them what happened and neither of them scolded me; in fact, they didn't say a word about it. I figured they were already aware of what was to come for me from Floressa.

The next day after school as I returned home, I fearfully walked into our apartment, because I noticed Floressa's car down in her parking space, and Dad's car wasn't in its space. Ada and Uche weren't scheduled to be back from school for another hour or so. I passed Dad and Floressa's bedroom to get to my bedroom to put my backpack away, and then went to greet Floressa in her room.

"Good afternoon, Mommy." I said.

"Who are you greeting?" Floressa asked in a harsh tone. "Eh? I said who are you greeting, Oma? Is it me?

The woman who is sleeping with another man? Eh?" she asked as she got up from her bed, and took quick strides towards me.

I stood in place in utter fear of what was about to happen, I held my arms up over my head and face, a normal reflex as Floressa struck me through my arms on my face, the hardest slap I had ever received from her in my life. I literally saw white dots suddenly appear, the equivalent of 'seeing stars.'

"Idiot! You scratched my face from my picture. Why didn't you scratch your daddy's face, too? Eh? Messing up my house...useless girl. 'A man asked you to tell me to leave your father,'" she mocked me, then suddenly she lunged at me again and struck me hard on my stomach with a closed fist. I crumpled to the floor in absolute pain; the wind was completely knocked out of me, and I couldn't even cry.

"C'mon, get out of my room, you useless girl! Idiot! Olodo! (*An insult; an uneducated person*) Mchwwwwww!!" she cursed me and gave a long hiss as I crawled out of her bedroom into the hallway. She slammed her bedroom door just shy of my feet and I lay in the hallway for what felt like forever before I could get up again. I didn't tell Dad what happened; what was the point? I simply told Ada and Uche that she beat me

155

after they asked if I was ok when they came home. I went to bed early that evening.

One Saturday morning some months later, Dad had a few errands to run and he took me along with him. It was nice having moments alone with him because we didn't go out often. Mommy Floressa and Dad worked a lot and my sisters and I were getting used to the schooling system here.

"What are those scars on your knee?" Dad asked while he was driving, looking over at my legs. I glanced down at my knees at the direction Dad was looking. I had on blue jean shorts and a black tee-shirt with a picture of Michael Jackson on it. "Are all those from riding your bike?"

"No! That's from Mommy Floressa!" I replied, not initially realizing what I had said until seconds after the words had come out of my mouth. Dad glanced over at me with a confused look on his face. I then realized that was the very first time I had mentioned any kind of abuse from Floressa. My sisters and I had gone our whole lives without once telling Dad that Floressa had been beating us every time he wasn't around and threatened our and Dad's life if we ever told.

"Floressa?" Dad asked, perplexed. "What do you mean? What happened?"

I hung my head down while Dad pulled the truck over, and I told him EVERYTHING! Dad cried.

That year, Dad and Floressa's marriage ended; it was 1992. Dad and Floressa's marriage wasn't exactly a peaceful one either because they frequently fought, even before I revealed to Dad her abuse towards us, but I don't believe Dad was able to trust her to be alone with us girls again. Dad only left the house when he needed to, like going to work, and even then, he'd call the house several times a day checking in on us and making sure he spoke with me before he hung up. And the days he didn't work, he took us with him when he was able to. The revelation of his wife's behavior must have sent his feelings for her over the edge. Floressa moved out of the apartment a few months later and for several months, it was just me, Dad and my sisters.

Dad now needed to travel for his importing and exporting business. One day, he told his siblings who lived a few minutes away from us that he needed to travel soon and would need their help for just two weeks keeping an eye on us girls. He assured them that they wouldn't need to do much because we girls were used to living alone since Nigeria and were now old enough to take care of ourselves during that time. Ada was fifteen, Uche was fourteen and I was thirteen years old. When we lived in Nigeria, Dad was used to leaving us girls alone in the house with either Mommy Floressa when she was there, or his brother and wife; who lived next door. They would check in on us every day and we'd go over to their house to eat our meals. Well, now we were living in the United States, Dad and Floressa had separated, and he still needed to travel, so he just needed someone to check in on us. After he assured us girls and his siblings he'd be back in two weeks, Dad left and my siblings and I were now alone in the apartment with about a three-week supply of food and one month's paid rent.

"Ada, I'm hungry!" I said to my sister as I held my tummy. We hadn't had a full meal in two days now and no one had come to check in on us this week. It was week four, and Dad still hadn't returned from his trip or phoned to tell us when to expect him back. Uche picked up the phone to call one of Dad's sisters, but no one answered the phone. There was a knock on the door and Uche went to open it.

"Hi, sweetheart!" A tall white man was at the door. "Is your father home?" he asked.

"He's at work," Uche lied.

"Do you know what time you'll be expecting him back today?"

"No! Maybe around 6 p.m." Uche replied.

"Ok, if you can, call him at work and let him know his rent is five days overdue and we need to get it today, ok?"

"Yes, sir," Uche replied and she quickly shut the door.

We three sat silently in the living room, with looks of despair on our faces. Uche went into our bedroom, came back out after a minute with her jacket on and started to leave the apartment.

"Where are you going?" Ada shouted behind Uche, but Uche was already out the front door and slammed it shut without a response back to Ada. A few hours later, Uche returned with some papers and a plastic bag in her hand.

"Where did you go?" Ada asked Uche as soon as Uche walked in.

"I went to apply for a job at McDonald's down the street.

"But you have to be sixteen years old to work in this country. Don't you know that?" Ada said.

"I know," replied Uche. "I told them I was sixteen and they interviewed me. I gave them our phone number, so nobody use the phone unnecessarily in case they call. She opened the plastic bag in her hand and handed me a pack of the mini chocolate-covered donuts. I was elated to see the donuts because I was so hungry. I began offering to share the donuts with them, but they both refused to take any.

"It's ok, Oma, you can have them. We're not hungry," Ada assured me.

The next day, Uche was out again looking for a job, and Ada was in the kitchen trying to put something together for us to eat. The phone rang. I ran over to answer it and it was Dad's other younger sister Aunty Nneka.

"Oma?" Aunty Nneka sounded frantic.

"Yes, aunty!" I hurriedly replied.

"Are your sisters there?" she asked.

"Yes," I replied not wanting to tell her Uche wasn't home so as not to get her into trouble for leaving the house.

"Ok, listen to me very carefully, you and your sisters need to pack a few of your clothes and get on the bus and come to my house now! Now...now...now! Are you listening?"

"Yes Aunty, I am." I replied with a bit of confusion in my voice.

"If anyone knocks on the door, don't open it. Don't open the door for ANYBODY! Do you hear?" Aunty Nneka asked again.

"Yes, Aunty." I replied as fear now began to grow in me.

"Ok, I'm at work but will be home soon to see you girls. I expect you there within the next thirty minutes, and I will call my house to make sure you guys made it in, ok?"

"Yes, Aunty," I replied. I quickly hung the phone up and told Ada what had happened.

"Did she say why?" Ada asked me.

"No! She just said we had to leave right now and that she was waiting for us," I replied.

"Ok, let's start packing, and maybe Uche will be back by the time we're done packing."

I packed a few clothes into my back-pack and Ada packed some clothes for her and Uche so we could leave as soon as Uche got back. We waited for Uche for another twenty minutes, but she still hadn't returned.

"We have to go. We'll leave her a note and call her when we get to Aunty's house to meet us there," Ada said. She wrote a note for Uche and left it on the coffee table, and we left the apartment.

We walked to the bus stop, and got on the bus we knew went to Aunty Nneka's house. We arrived at her town-house in fifteen minutes. Aunty Nneka wasn't home yet, but her two kids and babysitter were home.

Ada walked straight to the telephone and dialed our home number.

"Hello? Uche? Did you see the note we left you?" Ada listened for Uche's response, "Then why are you still there? You need to leave and come here right now!" Ada said sternly to Uche. "I don't know, you'll find out when you get here. Just leave and don't open the door for anyone." Ada was most likely responding to Uche questioning her about what was going on.

Uche sometimes liked to challenge Ada; not in a disrespectful manner, but in a 'I know what I'm doing and I don't need you to tell me what to do' manner, which often pissed Ada off, and this seemed to be one of those moments.

About two hours later, Uche came bursting through the door and looked terrified. Ada could tell something was wrong,

"What happened?!" Ada ran over to Uche who was still standing in front of the closed door.

"They almost got me!" Uche worriedly replied.

"WHO?" Ada asked.

"Right after I got off the phone with you, there was a knock on the door, and my heart jumped. I tip-toed towards the door and looked through the peep-hole and saw a man and a woman standing outside the door.

They kept knocking as if they knew I was there. When I didn't open the door, I thought they had finally left, but they didn't leave. They went and sat in their car outside. I was watching them through the window, and they waited in their car for over an hour. I waited and waited and waited, and then later they drove away. As soon as they left, I put on my shoes and ran out of the house to come here!" Uche replied hurriedly while clearly out of breath. "I ran from the bus stop here because I wasn't sure if they were following the bus to get me!"

Ada pulled Uche towards her and gave her a quick hug and soon afterwards said, "Next time, listen to me when I tell you to do something and don't be so stubborn. Thank God they didn't take you!"

"Those were people from CPS." Aunty Nneka told us after she got home.

"CPS?" I asked.

"Yes. Child Protective Services. It seems someone had called them and told them you girls were staying in the apartment by yourselves. Your step-mom called me telling me she received a call from them and that she wasn't going to go get you guys. So I had to make sure they couldn't take you girls, because if they did, it would be hard to get you guys back."

I noticed my two sisters exchange looks while I was

still confused about what CPS was, and why they wanted to take us.

About 7 p.m. that same evening, Dad's siblings all got together at Aunty Nneka's house to have a family meeting about my sisters and me. They put my father on speaker-phone while they were discussing what was to happen with us now. Who was going to be the one to take care of us until Dad got back?

"Christian!" Dad's immediate younger sister Nkechi shouted. "When are you coming back?" she asked.

"I don't know yet. I don't have money for a return ticket yet," Dad calmly responded.

"So, you bought a one-way ticket to Nigeria when you were leaving? That means you knew you weren't coming back, right?" Aunty Nkechi continued to ask, yelling at the top of her lungs in anger, as Dad stayed silent. "Ok, well, nobody here has money to take care of three teenage girls so we have to send them back to Nigeria!" Aunty Nkechi said.

"They can't come back here," Dad replied "The courts seized their American passports, and they cannot leave the country until they are eighteen-years old."

There was a long silence between the siblings. My sisters and I sat on the couch, listening to all the turmoil.

"Come and talk to your daddy! Come and ask him

what he wants us to do with you girls!" Aunty Nneka shouted in our direction. Uche got up and walked closer to the phone.

"Daddy! When are you coming back!?" Uche asked with anger in her voice.

"I don't know, Uche. Daddy is sorry."

"So what are we supposed to do now!? Where are we supposed to go!? Who is supposed to take care of us now!?" Uche shouted. Dad was silent yet again.

"Send them to foster care," Aunty Nkechi said, while throwing her hands up in the air. "Yes! Because they can't stay with me. I have a family of my own to take care of, Nneka has her own family, Floressa isn't going to take them, their mother just dropped them off a few months ago in the middle of the night, so we know she's not going to take them, their father doesn't want to come back and take care of them, so why should we be the ones to be burdened with them?" Aunty Nkechi continued.

"No, no, no. That's not an option, Nkechi," Aunty Nneka said. "If they are put in foster care, they will end up being separated."

The meeting went on for hours more with different ideas being thrown around and rejected. Finally, Aunty Nneka made a suggestion they all agreed with (well, almost all).

"Let's do this. Oma is still just thirteen-years old and hasn't started high school yet. There is a junior high school very close to my house here. She can stay here with me and walk to school from here, and Ada and Uche can go and stay with Chuks, since he doesn't have any of his kids here and lives alone. They can even help him with the cooking."

Uncle Chuks was the oldest of all my father's siblings; he was married and had six children, but his family were all living in Nigeria at the time while he worked here. He had been quiet the whole time as he was a man of very few words and was known only to speak when necessary. "Mba!! [*No*] No way! They cannot stay with me. I'm too busy, I work long, crazy hours and I don't have the time to be checking in on them when I'm not home. This is not a responsibility for a man. A woman has to be home to make sure they are well taken care of," Uncle Chuks protested. But after the rest of the family members spent ample time convincing him to take my sisters and assuring him it would be temporary, he finally succumbed to their pleas. I stayed with Aunty Nneka for one year while I attended 8th grade, while Ada and Uche moved in with Uncle Chuks and attended high school. Dad never permanently returned from Nigeria after he left.

Thirteen

Age 24 - 33

It had been several weeks since I had found out about my husband's infidelity. I didn't bring it up and Sebastian had developed an anger towards me since then. That was a new behavior he had developed; a sort of defensive barrier he'd adopted since the previous year. He walked around the house like *HE*, was angry at *ME*. I couldn't believe it; the nerve. I knew he was just waiting for me to bring up the issue so he could burst out all the defenses he must have come up with since our talk. He had become a master at trying to turn the tables on me and he had been successful many times before. But, as much as I'd wished he would have at least come and asked for my forgiveness for what he'd done, I knew his ego wouldn't allow him to.

"Am I not worth an 'I'm sorry' from him?" I cried to Victor over the phone, upset that it has been two months and Sebastian and I still hadn't spoken. "*He* broke our trust, *he* hurt me, *he's* the one who hasn't bought me flowers or celebrated my birthday in over two years. He used to take me to my favorite seafood restaurant in the city after he'd buy me flowers and gifts for my birthday! He used to buy me anniversary and Christmas gifts. We used to go out on spur-of-the-moment dates; we used to talk to each other about anything and everything. And now, now that I had found out that he's been cheating, he still hasn't even tried to fix it."

Victor listened silently on the phone. I had rambled on for almost an hour about all the pain I had and how difficult it was for me to see myself in that situation. Why wasn't I strong enough to just leave him? Why had I let him control my emotions like that?

"Oma, I don't think you know how beautiful and strong you are," Victor said to me. He had been quiet all this time and he had always told me since I started complaining about my marriage to him that he couldn't believe I was the same independent woman he went to school with.

"Oma, I rarely have any regrets in my life, but my only one true regret is that I didn't pursue you while we were still in high school. I've been attracted to you since then, but you had always been in a relationship."

Oh my goodness! Victor and I had always had some harmless flirtations here and there over the past few months, which I had been enjoying, but things just seemed to have gotten REAL. I thought to myself.

"And when you got in this relationship, I never knew it would lead to marriage so quickly. I kept waiting for my turn to be your man, but that turn never came. Oma, this man does not deserve you. I deserve you!"

Dead silence on the phone. I absolutely did not know how to respond to Victor right then. I had gone from snot-nose boo-hooing to total shock. Yes, deep down I knew Victor always liked me, but I also knew our friendship was a *safe* one because we were both married, and I had never been one to ever consider being unfaithful to Sebastian. It was a *safe* friendship for me because he knew me and every flaw about my character and it didn't seem to matter to him and I believe I knew his as well.

"Oma? Are you still there?" Victor asked after what seemed like a long silence.

"Hummm...ye...yes, Victor I am." I softly replied.

"Well?..." Victor asked. "What do you think about what I just told you?"

"Victor, you have been such a wonderful friend to me all these years and even a better one these past few months since I've been going through all this. I don't want to risk our friendship, Victor. And honestly, I'm afraid of losing you. But you're married with children, and *I'm* still married. No matter how bad my marriage seems right now, I can't replace a wrong with another wrong; I just can't. I do care very much about you, Victor, you must know that." I could hear him take a deep breath. "Victor, please tell me you can understand what I'm saying," I said.

He was silent for a few seconds. "Of course, I understand, Oma. I just had been holding these feelings in all this time and it never seemed to be the right time to tell you how I felt. You were either super-happy in your marriage earlier on, or you were angry or sad like you are right now over him and it's hurting me hearing you in all this pain from someone I know doesn't deserve you. No matter what, Oma, know that I will always be here for you. I understand that you may not feel the same way I do, but I just needed you to know how much I care about you! Yes, of course, we can remain friends."

Phew, I thought to myself. It was never easy for me to turn down a good man, and especially what Victor had come to mean to me these past few months; he had literally become my best friend. But no matter how badly Sebastian was treating me and handling our marriage, I was not even close to considering a divorce or leaving him.

Growing up, I had always heard that marriage was a lot of hard work, and even *WHEN* (because I was told it would happen) your husband cheats, never leave him for the other woman after you've put in all the work grooming him. I'd heard there were only three good reasons to leave a marriage; if he was *abusive*, openly *cheated* on you (where he acted nonchalant about it and everybody knew about it, causing humiliation), or a *lazy* man who didn't care to provide for his family. Otherwise, fight for your marriage no matter how bad it may get. That was the advice I got from my African aunties, and that was what I was holding on to.

Victor and I spent the next few weeks after our talk catching movies and having coffee and doing regular friends stuff, and it had helped get my mind off the issues I was dealing with at home.

One Saturday evening, Victor and I had gone out to a bar with some of his co-workers to celebrate his work promotion. We were all doing shots for every year he had worked for his company. It was my first time ever doing shots, as I was hardly a drinker. And Victor had been with his company for over twelve years. Well, let's just say, I didn't get past his first three years. I was clearly drunk after just the third shot and was quickly labeled the "lightweight" of the group (whatever that meant) and barely able to take a few steps without almost falling to the floor.

Weirdly enough, I was still somewhat self-aware of what was happening, but yet couldn't control my normal body movement; it was quite a different and exhilarating feeling. Victor held me up as we left the bar and walked to his car. He helped me get in the passenger seat, fastened me up in my seat belt, lowered the seat back, and shut the door. He went around and got in on the driver's side, he looked over at me, and I turned my head to look at him and we both smiled at each other in silence. I suddenly felt warm all over and a looking at his face, he seemed to desire me and I him; I sat up from my seat, slowly began to lean over to him, and I kissed him.

I pulled away a little to see his reaction, I had just

wanted to feel something other than the pain I had inside and Victor was my perfect man right then. He placed his hand on my face and softly kissed me again, then we began kissing each other passionately. He released me from my seat belt, ran his hand up my blouse and cupped my breast. I pulled him even closer to me, almost having him on top of me. He reached under my dress and began pulling my silk panties down my legs, past my knees; he ran his hands back up between my legs and gently caressed me between my legs, used his fingers and gently entered me; I moaned and thrust my body more on him. He then stopped kissing me just shy of my face, pulled his hand out and up from under me and licked his fingers.

"And you taste good, too," he said with a coy smile. I blushed at the intensity it had reached. We began kissing again, he pulled me up further on the seat as if to begin to go down on me; I suddenly felt guilt overcome me. *DAMN IT!!* I started to pull away, gently pushing him off me.

"Stop...stop...we need to stop...I can't, Victor...I'm so sorry," I said softly, a little short of breath. Victor leaned back into his seat on the driver's side, took in a deep breath and gently nodded his head as I pulled my panties back up. He didn't appear to be upset, though maybe disappointed, but I simply couldn't do this. This wasn't who I was as a person, nor who I wanted to become.

Even though Sebastian and I hadn't made love in months, and I was horny has hell, especially coupled with alcohol, it still didn't feel right. Victor was married and I knew his wife would be devastated if she ever found out about this because she clearly trusted our friendship. She certainly didn't deserve the same heartbreak I was going through.

My saving grace and strength that evening was that I had a friend in Victor who seemed to clearly understand why I had to pull away. As he drove me home, he occasionally stared at me as if to make sure I was ok. We didn't say much to each other during the ride. We pulled up in front of my house, he quickly came out of the car before I got a chance to begin opening my door and came around to my side and opened my door, held my hand as I got out, and asked, "You ok, Oma?" He seemed concerned that I was angry. And I was, but not at him.

"Yeah! I'm good. Thanks, Victor!" I responded, not needing to elaborate on my gratitude. Victor nodded silently and softly kissed me on my cheek.

Fourteen

AGE 4 - 13

Staying at Aunty Nneka's house was the first time in my life I had been without my sisters that long. It was also the year I was basically forced to become more mature and independent. I was used to leaning on my sisters to make decisions for me, tell me what to do, fight any battles for me, and basically take care of me.

Aunty Nneka was a cheerful woman; she had never gotten married, but had been dating a white-French man, Uncle Spence, for over nine years and they had two boys, Julius who was nine and Paul who was seven. I hadn't known my Aunty's family before this, but vaguely remembered the first time she introduced him to the family nine years ago, it was the topic of that year at family gatherings that she was dating a white man. Aunty's family seemed to run on a routine schedule; uncle Spence and Aunty Nneka both left for work in the mornings as soon as the babysitter arrived at 7 a.m, who then drove their kids to school. My new school was about three blocks away from the house, so after I was shown how to get there when I was registered, I walked to and from school with ease.

I got along with my cousins just fine, and after school I'd help them with their homework, though they hardly needed much help because they were quite intelligent for their ages. Besides missing my sisters very much, nothing spectacular happened around Aunty Nneka's home. For once it was actually *nice* not having anything happen, though it still felt somewhat foreign to me that one issue or another wasn't coming up. Almost daily my first few months there, I thought to myself that this must have been what having a real family was like, having and following daily routines, having breakfast and dinner together, doing homework right after school, being assigned a daily chore to be responsible for, being complimented when a task or assignment was completed well and so on.

I slept on a pull-out bed in the living room because it was only a two-bedroom town-house; the boys slept in one room and Uncle and Aunty slept in the other. I actually loved sleeping on the pull-out bed because it was the very first time I had ever seen a bed come out of a couch. I was fascinated that a whole bed had been produced from a small couch.

About six months into living with Aunty Nneka and her family, there were several mornings I woke up feeling uneasy about the dreams I had the nights before. I had dreams that someone was touching me 'down there' and it was a different feeling because I had never felt it before. The dreams weren't bothersome enough to disrupt my school-work or call my sisters to tell them about it, but they were so unfamiliar to me. Nonetheless, I thought nothing of it.

One night, for some reason, I was having a tough time falling asleep and it was very late at night, so I just lay in bed with my eyes closed, hoping that sleep would come eventually. I then heard footsteps coming out from Aunty Nneka's room. I shut my eyes real tight because I didn't want to get into trouble for still being awake so late. I listened as the footsteps got closer and closer towards my bed, possibly Aunty Nneka checking to make sure I was really asleep.

Suddenly I felt a hand reach from under my blanket, tactically pulling the elastic band of my pajama pants away and a little down from me, then reach into my underwear, and started touching me 'there'. What was happening? This was like the dream I'd been having. My heart started beating fast and I was scared to 'wake up' because I wouldn't know how to confront what was happening.

I quickly shifted my position without opening my eyes, as if I were about to wake up, hoping it would stop, and the hand was quickly removed and I heard footsteps start to quickly walk away. I squinted one eye open in the direction of the sound and I saw Uncle Spence standing just before the short hallway leading to his room, looking in my direction to see if I had woken up. I quickly changed my position to lie on my belly in case he decided to come back after I fell asleep again. He didn't come back; I knew he didn't because I didn't fall asleep for the rest of the night. I stayed up all night wondering why this was happening to me again, why I have always been in situations like these, and I was mostly wondering whether or not to tell my Aunty Nneka what had happened.

I wondered what might happen if I did and what might happen if I didn't. If I did, she might not believe me, and they might send me to that 'foster care' my Aunty Nkechi had mentioned during the family meeting. She might end up leaving him and it would be all because of me coming to live with them in the first place. I could be ridiculed by the family if she told other family members what had happened, and they could place blame on me.

I mean, there wasn't a possibility that didn't cross my mind. I then considered *not* saying anything, but when I thought about that option the only feeling I got was fear. I realized that this night wasn't the only time he had done this to me; those nights I had 'dreams' about it weren't dreams at all, which meant that more than likely he would do it again another night. I didn't want to have to stay up every night for as long as I lived there to pretend to be asleep and shift around in bed to deter him. So, I made the most comfortable decision for me; and that was to tell Aunty Nneka in the morning no matter what happened.

It was early Friday morning and the boys were getting ready for school as usual. After I folded my bed back in the couch and put my blankets away in the closet, I slowly began walking towards Aunty Nneka's room. My heart palpitated with each step I took. When I got to the door of their room, it was about a third of the way ajar and I stood there and started to tremble. I wasn't aware that my body was shaking until I raised my hand to knock on the door and noticed it was shaking; my heart was palpating at unimaginable speeds. I finally knocked.

"Come in!" Aunty Nneka said as she sat on the edge of her bed, pulling rollers out of her hair.

"Good morning Aunty." I greeted her and noticed Uncle Spence walk into the master bathroom.

"Good morning, my dear. How are you?" she replied.

"Fine," I said and hung my head down.

"What's wrong?" Aunty Nneka asked. She must have noticed I wasn't looking too comfortable. I stood there silently for a while looking for the words to start to tell her.

"Oma! What's the matter?" She suddenly had an uneasy tone in her voice, and she stopped pulling the rollers out.

"Aunty, I have to tell you something, but I'm afraid to say it." I began to talk with my words noticeably soft and shaky.

"Oma, you don't have to be afraid. You can tell your aunty anything. Now, what is the matter?"

I finally began. "The past few weeks, I have been

having these dreams that someone has been touching me…down there…" I pointed to my vaginal area "…but then last night, when I was in bed, Uncle Spence came to my bed and he started touching me there. I didn't know what to do, so I pretended to stay asleep after I shifted in bed and he left. Then later that's when I knew it wasn't a dream I had been having." I got all the words out as fast as I could. I noticed Uncle Spence's shadow in the bathroom moving about initially, then it suddenly stop, but he didn't come out of the bathroom. I knew he could hear me, but he never said anything while I was standing there. Aunty Nneka's position on the bed allowed her to look directly into her bathroom and she stared at her husband in silence and then I heard Uncle Spence softly say, "That's not true. I don't know what she's talking about."

Aunty Nneka just kept staring in his direction without uttering a word to him or me. I slowly backed out of their room and shut the door. What was to become of me now?

AGE 24 - 33

Two weeks had passed since I last spoke with Victor. He had tried calling, texting and emailing me, but I couldn't find the courage to answer or reply him because I knew we would have to address that night and I was not ready to. I was just not ready. Well, quite honestly, I was not responding because I had started having strong feelings for him.

Since that night, I had been spending most of my days re-living our kiss in the car, re-living how alive my body felt, how his body felt on mine, how soft his lips were on mine, how his desire for me made me feel like a woman again. I mean, there wasn't a moment I was not thinking about it. I thought, maybe I should have kissed him just a bit longer, or maybe allowed it to go the distance to see how he was in bed; was he a take-charge type of lover, or the gentle and smooth kind? Was he a giver or receiver? Would he have cared if I came, or was he the type to have just cared about himself?

I thought about what our lives might have been like if we both left our spouses. Would I have been happier? Could he have been the one who got away? My thoughts about him made me look at him in a different light - his smile, his laugh, his confidence, his charisma. I didn't know what to do with those feelings and thoughts; but knew I was still very much in love with Sebastian, even though he wasn't quite acting like he even cared about me.

On one of my gym work-out days, about 5:12 a.m., I was running the treadmill. I had on the earpiece from my cell phone listening to my work-out music: one of the songs I usually had on rotation to motivate me to run a bit longer and harder was Beyoncé's *I Care* because it made me angry with Sebastian:

"Cause I care...I know you don't care too much, but, I still care....la la la laaa la, baaby la la la la..."

It rang so true for me at that point in my married life, and it described the way I felt about my husband and how he was acting towards me. Beyoncé knew my pain for sure! The music was suddenly interrupted by a phone call from a blocked number. I was not used to getting phone calls that early in the morning, nor from blocked numbers.

"Hello?" I answered, sounding out of breath while still running the treadmill.

"Hi!"

I knew that voice instantly. My heart sank, my pulse went even higher, and my nerves started to get a bit rattled. I pressed the stop button on the treadmill, stepped down and paused for a second before I replied.

"Hi…hi, Victor, how are you?" Not knowing what to say past that. I felt he might be mad at me for avoiding him and I really wasn't prepared for that conversation right then. But I knew I couldn't just hang up on him or avoid him anymore.

"I've been better," Victor replied. "I've been trying to reach you, Oma."

"I know, Victor," I said, still out of breath. "I just needed a little time to think and, to be honest, Victor, I didn't know what to say. I would actually prefer it if we could speak face-to-face rather than on the phone like this. Is that ok?" I asked, hoping he'd be receptive to my request.

Victor was silent yet again for a moment and the silence made me more nervous because I couldn't see his face, and I couldn't tell if it was an *I'm mad at you* silence or an *I'm hurting* silence. I just needed to see his face.

"Sure, Oma. We can meet. Are you free for coffee today?"

"Yeah, I am. I can meet you at 7:30 a.m. at our usual spot. That sound ok?"

"Sure. See you then," Victor replied with a soft, yet sad undertone before he hung up.

I pulled the earpiece out of my ears. I couldn't work out anymore. *My heart might actually explode if it went any faster*, I thought to myself. I took a long drink of water from my water bottle, walked around the cardio area of the gym for a few minutes thinking. I could hear my music restart on my phone through the earpiece after we had hung-up. I pressed stop on my playlist, grabbed my towel, and headed out of the gym.

I arrived at the coffee shop ten minutes early, so I could find a perfect corner where we could sit and have a bit of privacy, and also allow me a bit of time to settle my emotions before he arrived as I'd been so nervous since we spoke. I ordered coffee for us both since I already knew how he took his coffee. Victor showed up exactly at 7:30 a.m. He had on a black wool coat over a gray turtle-neck, black jeans, and black shoes. As soon as he saw me, a slight smile appeared on his face.

He seemed more handsome that day than I could ever remember him being. I thought, *Was this how he had always looked? Damn! He's fine!* His skin was nicely tanned and smooth, his teeth seemed whiter, his shoulders seemed broader, and his walk seemed more like a glide. Ugh, I couldn't take it! I quickly looked away to hide my face for a moment. *Meeting him might not have been the best of ideas after all,* I thought to myself. I felt like if my skin were lighter, I'd definitely obviously be blushing; thank goodness I was dark.

"Hi, beautiful!" Victor said to me as he leaned down and kissed me on the cheek.

"Hey!" I replied. I wanted to reply 'Hey handsome,' but I felt that might have ignited something I was already trying to put out.

"You look wonderful as usual," Victor said as he sat down and removed his coat. "Oh, and I see you already got me some coffee. Thanks!"

"Of course," I replied with a wide smile, trying my best to sound as normal as we used to be "And you don't look too bad yourself." I took a quick sip of my coffee. We sat and briefly stared at each other with smiles on our faces, and then Victor took a sip of his coffee which broke our stares.

"Listen," I began "Victor, I just want to start off by apologizing for not returning your calls and texts. I just didn't know what to say and I was nervous. That night....ummm....that night was a wonderful night, Vic. We were celebrating your promotion, I met your co-workers and we were all having a good time. I also had some mixed feelings throughout that evening and I didn't know how to handle it. Vic, you know what I've been going through with Sebastian, and I don't want to do to your wife what Sebastian is doing to me." I stopped briefly, deciding to just let it all out once and for all. "Victor, I haven't stopped thinking about that night yet. I haven't felt so alive in ages. You made me feel beautiful the way you took care of me while I was obviously out of it…a little from the drinks. Yes, I know you've always kind of been a good friend when it came to my safety, but that night felt different. You are such a good guy and we've been such good friends all these years. I'm really just afraid of losing our friendship. What if we had gone all the way? What then? What would become of our spouses? Would you want to be that man to leave your family for another woman? I most certainly am not that woman; I couldn't leave Sebastian. And even *IF* I were to leave him, I most certainly wouldn't feel right leaving him for another man. I'm sorry, Victor. I hope I'm not rambling on and on, but I just want to make sure I get it all out before I hear what you have to say." I finally stopped and took a breath. I looked at my friend and hoped I hadn't broken his heart even more.

Victor had sat there listening to me the entire time; he hadn't even taken another sip of his coffee, and his eyes never left mine. His gaze seemed so loving, as if he were admiring me more as I spoke. My body was doing that thing again where I couldn't control it. Ugh!!

"Oma, it's ok. I completely understand what you're saying and I'm trying to respect it, I really am. It's just, I've been in love with you for so long, I honestly couldn't believe I finally got to kiss and hold you in that moment. I have also been thinking about that night, but I've been more concerned about how you were feeling after that. That's why I kept calling you. I wanted to make sure you weren't mad at me for taking advantage of you while you were a bit tipsy. It's just when I put you in the car and we stared at each other, you had a look in your eyes; like you wanted me the way I wanted you. So when you leaned and kissed me it was like a dream come true for me. I had wanted to kiss you many times before but never got the courage to. I wanted more of you so badly that night, Oma. You have no idea. Plus, you looked especially beautiful that evening. I yearned for you every time you laughed when we all were at the bar. You smelled so good, too. And as I was holding you when we were walking towards the car, your skin felt so soft. But after we kissed and then you stopped, I wasn't sure how you might have been feeling the next day." He stopped and took a deep breath. "Don't get me wrong, I love my kids and would never leave them and I know I have a beautiful wife and all, but that's kind of where it all ends for me. She's just beautiful; she doesn't seem to care too much about me or my feelings. She's always going shopping, buying things for herself, and never stops to ask me about my day. We've been growing apart for years, but I'm only staying with her because of the kids. But if you said to me today that you wanted to give us a try, Oma, I would leave this instant. That's how much I love you."

Boy, is he relentless. I thought to myself, but I was a bit uncomfortable with him talking about his wife with me, the woman he had having feelings for. I didn't want to be *that* woman. But I quickly realized that I had already become *that* woman, whether I liked it or not.

"Victor, I love you and you know that. But it's just not the same way you feel about me," I said, trying to convince both him *and* myself as I knew I couldn't really tell him I had starting feeling the same way. I honestly didn't want anything more to come out of our relationship. I was just not going to leave Sebastian, no matter how I felt. Period.

"I love our friendship, how free we are with each other, how we can talk to each other without any filters. I love that your wife is comfortable with our friendship and Sebastian is, well, semi-comfortable with you, but even then, we may have possibly lost that. I truly can't act on any feelings outside of our friendship, Victor. I hope you can understand?"

Victor leaned back in his chair, looked down, then away, taking deep breaths, and then turned back to me, "I do, Oma. I understand. Doesn't mean I like it, but I do understand. I'm at least glad I was able to get my thoughts out. Thank you for not letting me down too hard," he said with a smirk which in turn made me smile. The tension between us seemed to have subsided a bit. He leaned back over on the table and grabbed both my hands and gave them a good squeeze. We both smiled at first, then let out a small laugh between us. It was nice that we still had some innocence left in our friendship.

Fifteen

AGE 4 - 13

It wasn't too long after I had told Aunty Nneka what had happened that some of the other family members heard about it, and just as I thought, I had now been labeled 'a liar' and 'a home-wrecker,' and some family members were so glad that they never took me into their home. The week spring-session of 8th grade was over; I was quickly sent to live with Uncle Chuks and my sisters. I was ecstatic to be back with my sisters; we quickly caught up on everything and they supported me and encouraged me through my ordeal at Aunty Nneka's house. We spoke about it only once and never brought it up again. I don't believe the reason we didn't talk about it again was because we were trying to avoid the topic; I just felt we had gone through so much in our lives and were still going through so much, we didn't have much time to stop and sulk about this singular incident.

AGE 15 - 19

We stayed with Uncle Chuks throughout our high school years. Within a year of staying with Uncle Chuks, his wife in Nigeria heard he was now taking care of my sisters and me and grew upset that he wasn't taking care of his own children instead, so she sent all three of his kids, Obi, Izu and Nkem, here unannounced, and boy, did Uncle throw a fit about that. In under a year he had gone from living alone to having six kids, all under eighteen years of age, living with him in a two-bedroom apartment. A few months later, Uncle brought home a girlfriend who had three girls of her own. My sisters, cousins and I were all sitting in the living room late one afternoon and Uncle Chuks walked in the front door with them.

"You guys, this is Fatima. Make sure you help her with anything she needs. Her daughters will be staying here with us, too, so you all figure out your sleeping arrangements, okay? Uncle Chuks said to us.

"Yes Uncle/Daddy," We replied collectively.

Uncle Chuks must have already had the relocation ball in motion prior to the four additional people because, in under a month, we all moved to a house in the suburbs. At one given time, there were a total of nine children and two adults in one house. This arrangement, however, only lasted for a little while because my sisters and Obi applied and got accepted into different universities and soon left Uncle Chuks's house to school. Ada moved on campus attending an Ivy-League university on a financial-aid scholarship, and double majored in Microcell Biology and Chemistry. Uche, who moved over an hour away, also stayed on campus, and majored in social science. One of Uncle Chuks's sons, Obi attended a university away from home as well, and I attended San Francisco State University, which was close enough to go to from home. Not knowing what I wanted to major in initially, I decided to start off taking the required general education courses until I could find my niche. I found it two and half years into school in business management.

My stay at Uncle Chuks's house was almost peacefully uneventful until after my sisters had both left for college and I was yet again left alone without them to protect me as they always had. Fatima's kids, were raised a lot differently than we had been raised, so we butted heads often. They were used to doing what they wanted when they wanted, and I was used to asking for permission before I did anything. They'd get bad grades in school and walk around with an *I don't care attitude* after their mother attempted to confront them about it.

"How is getting a D in English the teacher's fault? This don't make no sense to me!" Fatima would say to the second-oldest girl.

"It ain't my fault. I told you that dude don't like me...dang! What you want from me?" she'd respond as she walked away.

It was quite unusual to me that they could get away with that sort of behavior. One of the girls was the same age as me, another was a year and a half younger, and the last was two and a half years younger. They weren't responsible or respectful, and I didn't like that they didn't care to take care of the new home we had moved to. They'd leave the bathroom disgustingly dirty after their shower; I used to gag whenever I went in after them. I often wondered how one can come out of the bathroom after a shower dirtier than when one went in. They'd go into a clean bathroom, come out, leaving their dirty clothes and used underwear on the floor, wouldn't put the cap back on the toothpaste after use, leave residues of the used toothpaste all over the sink, and never flushed the toilet. I mean, was this for real? How could you be girls and live like that?

I hadn't been used to telling anyone what to do, so

after I had asked them several times to clean up before they'd leave the bathroom, and I'd receive a sarcastic "Sure," I decided to just let it go. I changed my schedule to use the bathroom early in the mornings to avoid those sights. As time went by, I became more and more uncomfortable staying in the house. Fatima saw that her kids and I never got along, but as long as they were in good with her boyfriend's kids, I wasn't worth the effort to rectify any issue with them. I begun standing up for myself a bit more; they didn't seem to like that too much. I started getting threats from the girls.

"Bitch, if you don't get the fuck outta my room, I'mma kick your African ass!" the oldest of the girls would say to me after I'd told her to clean up her mess in the kitchen.

I wasn't a confrontational girl; I had never been in a fight before and didn't even know how to handle this type of behavior. I wanted to tell Uncle Chuks what was going on, but couldn't because I felt anytime I told someone that something bad was happening to me, I ended up getting blamed for it and removed from the home, so I made a decision to keep it to myself. But I was sure going to protect myself if anything were to happen; I made a decision to keep a knife in my room in case I ever got attacked.

In the meantime, I stayed away from any trouble, kept to myself in my room, and did as I was asked to. My weekly routine had become cooking for the house, cleaning up the kitchen and bathroom upstairs and half-bathroom downstairs, as well as vacuuming the two living rooms downstairs. It was my duty as the oldest girl in the house to make sure there was always cooked food for Uncle Chuks to eat, which I truly loved doing because he always complimented my cooking, and his compliments encouraged me to try something extra special the next time.

Uncle Chuks was such a hard-working man; he was barely ever home because he sometimes worked twenty-one-hour days for long stretches at a time. But sometimes when he'd come home, he'd go straight to my room very angry that the kitchen was a mess and the trash hadn't been taken out.

"OMA! Why are all those dishes in the sink? The minute I walk into the house, the first thing I'm smelling is garbage! There's trash all over the floor and counter! C'mon, go downstairs and clean up that mess. That's not what your uncle is supposed to be seeing after I come home from work!" Uncle Chuks would yell.

I was never given the chance to respond. I knew I always made sure the kitchen was clean after I cooked and before I went to my room, but with five other kids there, surely one or more of them had made the mess, but they never got yelled at 11 p.m. at night when Uncle came home. Uncle Chuks didn't know who made the mess or why it was there, nor did he care to know. All he knew was that his kitchen was dirty and it was always my responsibility and he was holding me accountable. Uncle Chuks wasn't the type of uncle one could *complain* to about an issue as trivial as keeping a kitchen clean.

With the feeling of being between a rock and a hard place and after two years of taking the brunt of the yelling from Uncle Chuks, I had had enough. It was time for me to stand up for myself and tell everyone that they had to do their fair share of the housework. And I also decided to make a time-line video recording of the house during a regular day to play for Uncle Chuks on his day off. That way he could see what I'd been trying to tell him all this time.

Well, to no surprise, my plan of telling the girls to do their share didn't go very well. Fatima's girls weren't the kind of kids that one told what to do. I think that was maybe what they wanted from me all that time; for me to confront them about their behavior because, as soon as I did, all three of them physically attacked me at the same time. I didn't know how to fight and there I was in my uncle's home and I was being stomped on the kitchen floor. I ended up with a broken index finger, a bruised eye socket, my upper lip split open, a bruised left arm and legs, and a large patch of my hair pulled out. I got up and quickly ran up the stairs to my room and locked the door. I called my sister Uche from my cell-phone and told her what was happening,

"I was just trying to get on video-tape the mess before I cleaned up, then I was going to clean the whole house, and was planning on taping the mess after. I was minding my own business videotaping and the small one came and asked what I was doing. I didn't answer her, then she went to get her sisters and they all came out asking what I was doing and as I was telling them exactly what I was doing, the oldest one started coming towards me cursing me out right up to my face. I pushed her away from me, and she and the other useless idiots started jumping me!" I cried to Uche.

"Did you call the police?!" Uche asked in hysterics.

"No."

"Get off the phone and call the police right now, Oma!! Those people cannot get away with jumping you...NO! Call the police right now and then call me back!"

Uche's school was over an hour's drive away from

home so she couldn't come right over. There was a knock on my bedroom door and it was my cousin Nkem who handed me the land-line.

"It's my dad; he wants to talk to you," my cousin said.

"Hello?" I answered the call.

"Oma! What's going on?" Uncle Chuks asked.

Apparently, one of the other kids had already called Uncle Chuks to tell him what happened, but I also told him my side of the story and that Uche asked me to call the cops and I was about to.

"Don't call any police to my house. Do you hear me?" Uncle asked.

"Yes, uncle," I softly replied. And then he hung up.

My cell-phone rang immediately after and it was Ada.

"Oma! Have you called the cops?" Ada asked; she clearly had already spoken to Uche and she was following up to make sure I called the cops.

"No! Uncle Chuks just asked me not to."

"Why? Did he say he was going to do anything about what happened?" Ada asked.

"No, he just asked me what happened, I told him, and when I told him I was going to call the police he told me not to and hung up."

Ada said ok and hung up.

About five minutes later a police patrol car pulled up to the house and my cousin came to my door telling me they were asking me to come down. I went downstairs to meet the cops. It seemed that one of my sisters went ahead and called the cops on my behalf because somehow they knew I wouldn't do it.

"Hello, ma'am! Are you Oma?" one of the officer's asked me.

"Yes, I am," I replied.

"You look pretty banged up there; are you ok? Do you need a medic?"

I held my upper lip to cover the gash and shook my head no. I was still afraid of what Uncle Chuks would do to me if he knew the cops were called, and I just wanted them to leave. I could see Uncle's girlfriend's kids looking out of their bedroom window at me talking with the cops.

"Ma'am, we got a call that there was an altercation going on here and you're clearly bruised up. Do you want to file charges against the people who did this to you?" the cop asked.

"No, I don't," I softly responded, hoping if I kept giving short answers they'd leave.

"Ok, well, give us a call back if anything changes,

ok?" he said and he and his partner got in their car and took off.

I walked back into the house and I could hear the girls giggling in their room as I walked up the stairs to my room. Forty minutes later and both Uche and Ada were in the house. I could hear them shouting downstairs. I run downstairs and I saw Uche shouting at Nkem.

"What were you doing while these rats were beating up your cousin?!" Nkem was about three years younger than me and she was a meek and quiet girl so I didn't expect much from her. Uche was very upset as she stood in front of Nkem.

"I was trying to stop them," Nkem replied.

"HOW?! By watching them and calling your dad on the phone?" Uche now seemed more disappointed in Nkem than angry. The other girls came and stood outside their bedroom door just waiting to be confronted, but my sisters didn't even look their way. Uche and Ada treated them as if they were not even in the room, walked right by them, most likely wishing one of them even uttered a word, which they didn't.

"Oma, let's go upstairs, you're leaving this house for these people. I know we don't have much in our lives but you don't deserve to be treated like this." Uche went on: "How can you be living in this kind of condition and you have family in the house, too, and they are just standing there watching you get beat? Would she do the same thing if it were her own sister?" Uche was clearly livid. Ada brought up a clean garbage bag and started to throw all my clothes and shoes in there. Ada was mostly an action kind of girl; she was going through my room with lightning speed packing all my things up.

"We don't have much, but we're going to be ok. You're going to stay with me until we can find somewhere else for you to stay!" Uche continued. In less than fifteen minutes, my sisters had packed all my things up. We all got into Ada's car and they took me away from Uncle Chuks's house.

Uche sublet an apartment for me for two months so I could get to school, while she was still paying for her other apartment by her school an hour away. But she could not continue carrying both payments past the two months as much as she tried to find the funds. I, on the other hand, did have a grocery store job at the time, but the job I had was close to Uncle Chuks's house that I used to walk to and was now too far away for me to get to, as I didn't have a car at the time. Uche asked one of her girlfriends to let me stay with her for a few days until I could find somewhere to live.

After about a month of sleeping on Uche's friend's couch and desperate for a home, I tried going back to Uncle Chuks, asking him if I could come back, and he told me no, that too much had happened and he wasn't happy with the way I left his house after all the years he had taken care of me and my sisters. I could only apologize to him for the way we had left, but was still disappointed that I wasn't worth being taken into his home again. He basically had chosen his girlfriend and her kids over me.

How could I blame him? Dad was the one who left us; he never sent any money to us, as far as I knew. He never called my uncles or aunties, thanking them for all their help with us. He never asked us how we were paying for college. He wasn't there to teach us how to drive. He wasn't there now that I was homeless. I was so angry and disappointed with my father, and through all my struggles my relationship with him grew further apart.

I constantly searched and applied for jobs and had to use Uche's friend's address on my job applications. I ended up staying on her couch for about two months. Ada got a job with the Horizon Milk Company in the microbiology department by that second month, and she rented a studio apartment for me. She paid two months' of my rent for me and within those months. I had finally gotten a part-time job and was on a full-time schedule in college. I also took out student loans to help buy a car, and so I was able to continue with the rent and other bills from then on.

Sixteen

AGE 24 - 33

Sebastian and I had pretty much been living as roommates the past few months. His ego wasn't allowing him to ask for forgiveness and he began to take my silence as blatant disrespect towards him. The previous week, I was hopeful that as my birthday approached he would have used that opportunity to do something nice and maybe reconcile with me, but my birthday came and went without so much as a birthday card from him. Well, he did say "Happy birthday" to me that morning when he woke up, even though the birthday wish was said under his breath; I guess that was something.

When I did try to speak with him on a couple of occasions to see if I could get the conversation going, we would end up arguing and most of the time in the arguments he would accuse me of not acknowledging him when I woke up in the morning, not making him meals anymore, not doing what I was supposed to do as a wife anymore. And I definitely didn't find it even remotely amusing that he wasn't remorseful for his actions and was trying to turn the tables on me. I felt my reaction towards his behavior was a normal reaction that any other woman who had been cheated on would have.

In fact, I felt it was way less subtle than what the average woman might have done. I was heartbroken, sad, and simply put, hurt. My heart broke every day he walked by me without talking to me; my heart broke every time he got dressed and walked out of the house and didn't tell me where he was going; my heart broke every time I texted him asking where he was and he didn't reply me.

But sometimes I didn't get too angry about his leaving because I'd find out he was hanging out with his friends doing their usual activities: drinking, gossiping and sometimes going out to clubs. Which again, I didn't mind, because Sebastian wasn't exactly an *any* girl-chasing kind of guy. He was more likely to get close to a woman he knew than a total stranger; not that that was impossible either, just less likely. Sebastian was more into hanging with the fellas and picking up the bill when they'd go out (which is another issue I had, only because they had started hanging out more often and it had starting getting expensive and was affecting our finances.)

Sebastian liked to be in control of his environment; he never let any of his friends pay for his meals or drinks. He once told me - *"I don't want to give anybody the opportunity to insult me tomorrow by saying they paid for my food or drink."* Sebastian was a proud man and he had a habit of never putting himself in positions to allow anyone to (as he put it) *insult him.* And those rules apparently applied to me as well; he just didn't like being confronted about his wrong-doings, and I was sure he wasn't apologizing to me because he figured I wouldn't let it go so easy and would expect him to admit being wrong and attempt to right that wrong. Frankly, a snowflake had more of a chance in hell than I had of ever getting that apology.

I once again had started to find serenity in my (now back to normal; or what seemed to be normal) conversations with Victor. We didn't hang out as often anymore, but I did call him every so often to talk about regular things, like work, kids, and such, and he'd tell me about his day and all. I could tell he had started letting me initiate the calls, not calling me as he once had, which, quite frankly, I was comfortable with and understood why he did so. Plus, I liked that he always answered my calls, he never let it go to voicemail and, if by chance it did, he'd called me right back. Every once in a while, Victor would ask how things are going with Sebastian, possibly to see if I was close to leaving him. But I didn't talk about Sebastian and my relationship anymore because it was awkward and I was sure Victor wouldn't want to hear about how Sebastian was treating me, so I'd just reply with, "Working it out."

Victor's and my relationship had clearly changed and, even though we both tried to get things back to where they used to be, it wasn't the same. It just seemed more torturous. So our daily phone calls quickly faded to weekly, then down to monthly, if that.

"Can we go see a marriage counselor?" I asked Sebastian while we both lay in bed one Sunday evening.

"For what?" Sebastian asked.

"Does our relationship seem ok to you? Is this how you want to spend the rest of our marriage?" I asked, trying to keep my voice steady and low, as I had once again initiated a conversation and I didn't want it to quickly turn left again.

"I don't see anything wrong; if this is how you want to continue acting in our marriage, making accusations, not greeting me when you wake up in the morning, not cooking for even the kids to eat, doing what you want…well, that's fine with me. Me, too, I can do what I want. You accused me of doing something that I told you wasn't what it seemed; you went and made phone calls to people you felt you could get better answers from before even asking me. You don't even know if that same woman has been trying to break up this marriage and you just believed everything she said and didn't even want to listen to me when I was talking to you," Sebastian said.

It was clear he was attempting to turn the tables on me; he had had months to figure out his defense. He created a response by presenting an anger towards my treatment of him, and now he was attempting to make me feel bad for even making the call to Nika, attempting to make me feel bad, indirectly calling me a bad mother by saying I wasn't cooking for the kids, which wasn't true; I just wasn't cooking for *him*. He was attempting to make me feel like a bad wife because I didn't "greet him" in the morning when I woke up. Hmmmm, it had never been a behavior of mine in all our years of marriage, for me to wake up in the morning and say to my husband: "Good morning, my husband." That just wasn't our marriage, and he knew it. At best, when I'd wake up most mornings, we'd flirt with each other a bit in bed, but was he seriously expecting me to have that same behavior in our situation? I knew what he was trying to do, but I didn't want the conversation to turn into another argument, so I just kept quiet and let him continue.

"Oma, I have tried my best for you. I have been leaving you all this time, watching to see what you would do, to see if you would even try to initiate a conversation, and all these months have gone by without us talking. Now you're asking me to go to a marriage counselor? No...I'm not going anywhere. If there is anything you want to talk about, we don't need anybody else, you can just talk and I'll listen."

I was honestly emotionally exhausted from all the months of silence and the continued heartbreak from his actions, and now his accusations towards me. I just didn't want to fight anymore. I wanted to move on, let it all go and, as I was taught, fix my marriage.

"Ok, Sebastian, that's fine. I'll accept that I called her before asking you first, I'll take that I haven't been cooking like I usually do and I'll take that I haven't been acknowledging you when we wake up, but I call that an *I was upset* behavior, simple. I didn't do all that to, as you put it, "disrespect you". You hurt me and I was waiting for you to come and fight for me, to fight for your marriage. But I'm not gonna argue about this anymore. This has gone on long enough and I'm exhausted. You're clearly not happy no matter how you may try to portray that you are, and I haven't been happy either."

My emotions started to flare up. "For God's sake, Sebastian, this whole thing almost drove me to having an affair with one of my best friends."

Sebastian quickly turned his head at me with a look of confusion on his face. *DAMN!* I hadn't meant to say that, but it just came out and I started tearing up, as I was suddenly overcome with emotions. "Thank goodness nothing happened but it easily could have. I've been so unhappy these past few years, Sebastian. We haven't been doing the same fun things we used to do. You used to take me out on surprise dates, I used to come home to you cooking meals for me, you used to rub my feet and asked how my day was, you used to pay attention to me and when all that stopped, I knew all that energy had to be going someplace else, which is why I called her. I'm a woman, Sebastian, and sometimes we women need a bit of attention from our men to let us know you still find us attractive. We need to know you would marry us all over again if you had a choice. I need to feel like I wasn't a mistake for you. I don't think that's too much to ask, I just want my husband back, the one who used to care. Do you still care, Sebastian?" I stopped, taking in deep breaths. I honestly hadn't planned on even saying much, I was ready to just say my 'yeses', 'no's' and 'I'm sorry's ' and move on.

"Who was this best friend you almost had an affair with?" Sebastian asked.

Really? After all I had just said he was still stuck on the 'almost affair' part? Typical.

I paused for a long time, initially not wanting to say Victor's name because I knew Sebastian would definitely confront Victor and would most likely forbid me from ever talking to Victor again, but I was also struggling with wanting to be honest with my husband now that we were talking things out. I felt we were in the midst of trying to start anew and if that meant sacrificing a friendship for my marriage, then so be it.

"Victor. But, like I said, nothing happened. Victor has been there for me all these months, Sebastian. He has been there for me while you and I hadn't been talking. He was my movie-going, coffee-drinking, how-was-your-day-asking friend. That's it." I said, attempting to minimize Victor's and my relationship.

"What exactly made it an almost affair, Oma? Did you guys have sex? What? What did you guys do?" Sebastian asked again, visibly upset and needing to know details.

"No, Sebastian, we didn't have sex, but we did kiss. It was an in the moment kind of kiss, not like we had planned it. We both had had a bit too much to drink and we quickly got carried away, and I think we both realized what we were doing and then we stopped and it hasn't happened since. There's nothing for you to worry about, Sebastian; he's married with kids. You know him, you know me. You know we wouldn't do anything to intentionally jeopardize our marriages."

It had now become a discussion of what *Oma* did wrong and apparently everything that Sebastian had done wrong was no longer the issue; that always seemed to happen to me. But we had to deal with it. Sebastian and I talked literally *ALL NIGHT LONG* about all the details of Victor's and my relationship. He wanted to know every detail. For the next three days, Sebastian called in sick from work and I canceled all my appointments with vendors for my upcoming events, and Sebastian and I stayed home and talked about every issue we had been having, From Victor to Nika, to financial issues and the works. By the end of those three days, we were both emotionally and physically drained and exhausted. There was a lot of crying, shouting, cursing, and eventually, calming down. It had been an emotional roller-coaster, but in the end; we got it all out and got to start over, somewhat.

Trust wasn't easy to just rebuild.

Seventeen

AGE 24 - 33

It was 2010. I came home from work. The house was dead quiet, which was quite unusual for a house with two small kids, a nanny and a husband. The nanny and kids weren't home and the whole house was dark; the only light on in the house was upstairs in our den which we had made a home office.

"Honey?" I called up to Sebastian.

"I'm upstairs, babe, come here!"

I walked up the stairs and as soon as I reached the top step, I heard my favorite song start to play:

"I must have rehearsed my lines a thousand times,
until I had them memorized, but when I get up the nerve,
to tell you the words, just never seem to come out
right…"

It was Patti LaBelle's *If Only You Knew*. But it sounded different; it didn't sound like it was coming from a CD player; it wasn't as clear.

I walked into the den and Sebastian had on a dark, two-piece suit and was standing next to what I had been asking him to buy me for years….a vinyl record player!

"Honey, I know we've had some quite difficult times these past few years and I know I haven't been the most supportive through it all, so I just wanted to first start off by saying…" He paused for a minute and appeared to start to choke-up, but I knew he wasn't going to cry because Sebastian wasn't the crying kind. "…I-AM-SORRY! I have blamed every hardship I've struggled with on you. I blamed you for not working and helping with the bills when you weren't working, even though I initially just wanted you to stay home with the kids. I then blamed you for spending too much time working when you began working. I blamed you for not spending more time with our kids and leaving all the work for our nanny and allowed myself to believe you were a bad mother. I resented you for not paying attention to me like you used to. You seemed to be always too busy for me."

Tears began filling-up in my eyes and I cried softly. My husband was saying all the things I had literally been dreaming and praying for. I fell to my knees, overcome with emotion as he continued.

"But I learned that I needed to stop and self-reflect. I asked myself, What exactly do I want from you, Oma as my wife? I have been asking myself this same question all week and I soon found that every answer I gave myself, you were already doing. Now, you may not have been doing it exactly as I expected, but I knew you were doing it according to what you had on your plate. I wanted a working wife, an attentive mother to her children, a wife who cooks, takes care of herself, and honey, even when you're just in sweats you look good." He chuckled. "I also want to be a better husband for you, Oma. I want you to be proud of me the way you used to be proud of me. I want you to trust in me, Oma, the way you used to put all your trust in me. I want you to look at me the way you used to look at me. Honey, I want to take care of you all over again, and I want us to start today! Tell me, babe, what do you want me to do to make you smile again?"

I was still on the floor on my knees, teary faced. It was like a romantic movie playing right before my eyes, and I wondered what the trigger could have been for him to suddenly realize all this. But it didn't matter to me; that moment, my husband was appreciating me and telling me what I had longed to hear.

"Sweetie, you've already done it," I responded.

Sebastian came over to me, lifted me up from the floor, hugged me tightly like he'd lost me and now he'd found me. We embraced while we slowly rocked to Ms. Patti singing my song. I never knew he had been listening when I told him this was my favorite song:

"...hummmm if... only you knew, how much I do,
do Loooove yooou
Ohhh if, only you knew, how much I dooo
do looove you Ohhhhh eeeeiiiff..."

Sebastian took my tear-filled face, wiped it with his hands, and softly began to kiss me. We kissed each other like we were in love all over again; I gently pulled away a bit confused.

"Honey, where are the kids?" I asked, because the kids had never slept outside the home before.

"They are with your sister Uche and their cousins. I

asked her to keep them for the night for us and I gave the nanny the night off. We can pick them up tomorrow afternoon and maybe take a family drive together to Monterey Bay and visit the aquarium; the kids will love that."

Sebastian walked me to our bedroom, and started the shower for me. "Take a quick shower, the night is still young." He walked out of our bedroom and closed the door behind him. I got in the shower and reminisced on what a wonderful surprise that was from him, and I smiled at how handsome he looked in the three-piece suit. He wasn't the suit-wearing type of guy, so I knew it took a lot for him to get the suit strictly for me.

After I stepped out from the shower and dried off, I walked into our bedroom, and there on the bed lay a brand new red dress. It sparkled like rubies and next to it was a ruby-red necklace. Sebastian must have laid them on the bed while I showered. I teared up again, not believing this was really happening to me. This was the kind of thing that I had only dreamed about and, quite honestly, when I had those dreams I never pictured Sebastian being the one to do this for me. Yet, here I stood in our home just marveling at his surprises.

I put on my favorite lotion which had an ever so

tiny hint of gold glittering in it, sprayed on my favorite perfume, and put on my best black silk underwear. This occasion clearly called for my one-carat diamond earring studs I had bought myself a few years back. I finished getting dressed, came out of the room and headed down the stairs. Sebastian was standing at the base of the stair-case looking up at me as I made my way down.

"THAT'S MY BABY!!" he said with the biggest smile on his face. He looked at me like he admired and adored me. When I made it down, he gently kissed my cheek and asked, "Are you ready for your night?"

I nodded my head, not sure where we were going, but was excited about the unknown. We walked out the front door as he held the small of my back, and, low and behold, yet another complete surprise: a black 4-door Chevy Suburban with a limo driver. The driver proceeded to open the door and assisted me into the car, and Sebastian entered after me. He handed me a single red rose. "I come in peace," he said jokingly as he sat next to me. "You're pretty quiet; you doing ok?" he asked.

I nodded my head. "Oh, yes. better than ok. Just a bit taken aback with all these surprises. I'm trying to think where you found the time to plan all this without me finding out," I replied.

"Well, that's not for you to worry about sweetie. Just let me take care of you tonight, ok?" he asked.

"Okay!" I replied.

We began our drive towards the city. While in the car we talked about how much we had missed each other, and some of the things he had struggled with. We talked about our future plans as a couple and as parents, we spoke like we were best friends again.

But for some reason the talk about our future was mostly coming from my end, and he just seemed to be going with it; he wasn't objecting to anything I was saying, but I noticed he wasn't adding to it either. I'd say how we both needed to take more family trips together with the kids, piggy-backing on his comment on our road trip to Monterey Bay, and his response was, "We'll see". I didn't want to read too much into it; I was enjoying my night.

Our first stop was one of my favorite restaurants which served seafood on the pier with a beautiful view of San Francisco's Golden Gate Bridge. I ordered a glass of Chardonnay, the grilled calamari for my appetizer, the chef's lobster special for my main course, and chocolate lava cake to indulge in. He ordered soup special and the Maine lobster.

After dinner, we headed to downtown San

Francisco to a Broadway show at the AT&T Park Theater. It was a Cirque du Soleil show. It was such a magical show, full of lights, acrobatics and so fun and fascinating to watch. I was like a kid in a candy store bursting with excitement.

Sebastian held my hand in his most of the night, caressing my fingers every now and then. I felt him glance over at me several times hold a smile on his face, likely because he could tell I was enjoying the show.

After the show, we walked to our chauffeured Suburban and the driver took us around the city for hours while we visited places we hadn't before. About 1:15 a.m we headed back home. We had had such a wonderful and long night, and we were both thoroughly exhausted. After Sebastian tipped the driver (handsomely, I must add), we walked into our warm home; we had left the heater on prior to leaving because it was a cold night. We went upstairs to our room, took off all our clothes, left them on the floor trailing towards our warm, soft, comfy bed, and we both fell on the bed and immediately fell fast asleep. But, I made sure he woke up to him in my mouth the next morning.

It was about 8:30 a.m. Sebastian and I had made love twice already that morning and now we lay next to each other with my head placed on his chest in bed.

"Babe, there's something I need to say to you," Sebastian said as he caressed my back. Wow, more words of admiration? A girl can get used to this, I thought to myself.

"I…I…" He was stuttering his words now. He sat all the way up in bed and took a deep breath. Oh, this can't be good. My heart fell, suddenly nervous at what he was trying to say. I sat up and turned to face him.

"Babe, I think we may need to separate for a little while, I think I am in love with someone else, but I also don't want to lose you. I just need some time to figure things out."

My heart sank.

Eighteen

AGE 24 - 33

It had been a month since Sebastian moved out of the house and I was starting to get into a single mom, single woman routine. I'd wake up and instead of rolling around in the bed a bit longer with a warm body next to me, I'd hop out of bed at 4:45 a.m. sharp so I could be at the gym by 5 a.m. I'd work out for about an hour, be home by 6:15 a.m., fully showered and dressed by 7:30 a.m. while the nanny helped get the kids ready for school. I'd drive the kids to school by 8 a.m. and set off to my office.

At work, I'd keep myself busy, taking on more

clients than usual, assisting some of my vendors with duties they most likely could have handled on their own. I'd call the nanny more times than usual, making sure the kids had enough to eat, and that there was nothing I needed to stop and pick up from the store on my way home.

It was about 6 p.m. on a Friday, and I was still sitting in my office finishing up a party design plan I had been working on all week to present to a client. My phone rang; on the screen it showed "HIM". What could Sebastian want from me? We had agreed only to text or email if either needed to communicate regarding the kids, and the only exception to calling directly was in an emergency. I told him that was the only form of communication I was willing to have with him.

I sent the call to voicemail; after all, the kids were at home with the nanny so it couldn't be a child emergency. Two minutes later, my phone beeped with a voicemail notification. *Humm...he left a two-minute message?* I thought to myself, while looking at my phone, contemplating whether or not to listen to the message. I opted not to listen to it till the next day. I refused to let him control how I was feeling anymore. I had just gotten myself into a routine, both emotionally and physically, and anything he had to say could shift my emotions. I was not ready for any kind of shift, positive or negative.

Driving home, I was listening to one of my soothing CDs:

" *When we met…always knew….I would feeeeel the magic for yooou…*
on my mind….constantly, In my arms is where you should beeee;
I love you here by me, baby;
You let my love fly freeeee,
I want you in my life for all tiiime….la la la la la laaaa
Caught up in the rapture of looove,
nothing else can comparrre,
when I feel the magic of yoooou… "

Anita Baker songs always calmed and relaxed me. I started to reminisce on when I fell in love with Ms. Baker; I used to make love to one of my first loves to Anita Baker music, and he was a good lover, too. *Boy, did he know how to hit the spot with me. Whatever happened to him anyway*? I thought to myself, now sitting at a red light. My phone rang and it was Uche calling.

"Hello?" I answered.

"Hi, sis!" Uche said.

"Hey, sis! How are you?" I asked.

"I'm good; I'm just calling to check in on you. You doing ok? I haven't heard from you in weeks now, been a bit worried."

I stayed silent on the phone contemplating what to say, how much to say. I was not in the mood to talk about Sebastian, I was not in the mood to discuss why I hadn't called or returned phone calls, and I wasn't in the mood to explain, either. But I also wanted to get all those bottled up feelings out and Uche had always been there for me. I had told her when Sebastian left, but hadn't spoken to her since.

"Yeah, everything's ok. I'm just heading home right now. You doing ok, sis?" I responded, steadying my voice so she couldn't tell I was upset. The sound of her voice always reminded me of love, of companionship, of being thought of, and I had been functioning so far without a need for companionship.

"Yeah, I'm fine. And stop trying to change the subject back to me, Oma. I need to know how you are. Are you almost home? Would you like to stop by my place before going home? I'll order Thai."

"No. Not tonight, Uche. I have a meeting with a big client in the morning and I still need to finish up on some last minute details. Can I take a rain check?" I lied about the meeting, hoping she didn't push much harder, because if she did, I would crumble to pieces and just give in.

"Sure, sis! We can catch up later then. Can I come over early evening, then, with the kids? Maybe we all can go to the park and let the kids play around for a bit. Sound good?" Uche asked.

"Sure," I responded.

"Ok, I'll give you a call tomorrow to confirm a time. I love you, sis!" Uche said.

"Love you, too sis!" I responded.

I drove in silence for a few minutes, then decided to listen to Sebastian's message.

"Hi, Oma. It's Sebastian. I know you said we shouldn't call each other unless there was an emergency with the kids, but I needed to talk to you. I'm not sure if you are free tonight but I'd really like to see you tonight if you are available. " He paused for a bit, his voice sounded sad, and desperate. "I'll try you again at 8 p.m. Please answer."

I guess he didn't leave a two-minute message; there was more silence on the message than there is a 'message'. I looked at the time and it was 7:52 p.m.; I had all of eight minutes to decide whether or not I was going to take his 8 p.m call. I was certain I didn't want to talk to him, but was also curious as to what he had to say. I recalled our last conversation:

"I think I am in love with someone else…" Yeap! That's what he had said to me right after he had taken me out on a romantic night, right after he had made love to me that same morning, knowing full well what he had planned the whole time. What kind of human being was that? If that wasn't the epitome of selfishness, I wasn't sure what was. I never confronted him that day. I didn't ask him who 'she' was; I already had an idea. I didn't ask him how long it had been going on. I didn't ask him why he was doing that to his family. I just refused to give him the satisfaction of reciting any answer he may have already prepared leading up to that moment. If he wanted to go be in love with someone else, he was going to have to just go and be with her and not explain to his satisfaction why he was doing it. But the only thing I did tell him when he was all packed up and leaving:

"Don't think you're the only one who needs to find love, I won't be waiting for you." And I meant it at that time. I had thought about calling up some of my exes; I had thought about calling Victor and taking him up on his offer. I thought about reinventing myself and dating more than one man at a time and planned on having fun with it by having one man for Wednesdays and Friday evenings, and another for Thursdays and Saturday evenings. I just let my mind run free the first few days Sebastian was gone. I tried not to let *his* decision to leave affect *my* feelings.

Why must I cry? He was the one who wanted to leave. Why must I feel like I did anything wrong, when all I'd done was humanly right. I allowed myself to use 'humanly right' because of course I hadn't done everything perfectly as a wife but as close to perfect as humanly possible.

But it had been over a month since Sebastian left and I was yet to do any of the things I said I'd do. I had just buried myself in work and my kids, and refused to talk to anyone about my feelings.

"*Ring, ring*" my cell phone interrupts my thoughts. "HIM" is calling. I glanced over at the time on my dashboard and noted it was exactly 8 p.m. What to do? What to do? As the phone rang into the third ring, I decided to go ahead and answer might as well just get it over with. "Hello?"

"Hey, Oma, how are you?" Sebastian sounded a bit taken aback on the other end; I guess he wasn't expecting me to answer.

"What's up?" I responded coldly, not wanting to get into any formalities with him. He wasn't going to get anything easy from me ever in life again. Not even a greeting.

"I'm glad you answered. I was hoping you and I could get together sometime this week."

"Get together for what, Sebastian?!" I responded, frustrated.

"Oma, I want to come home. I miss you, I miss the kids, our house, and I miss us. I was just hoping we could sit and talk about that possibility. Please, Oma...please!"

"Are you fucking kidding me, Sebastian!?" I snapped. What did he think this was - a revolving door? "I can't...I can't with you right now, Sebastian! You don't get to come and go as you please. You don't get to decide when you need a break and when you're done having a break. You don't get to throw tantrums whenever you want and expect all will be well with just an apology. No! You stay right where you are and be happy there. You told me you were in love with someone else, right? Well, Sebastian, be in love with her, and stay with her. Did I ask you any questions when you were leaving? Did I beg you to stay? Have I called you since you've left? So what gives you any impression that I want you back? Nope. Stay where you are. I'm not done being in love with the guy I'm in love with right now. So when I'm done being in love with him, *I'll* give you a call and let you know." I hung up.

The nerve! I wasn't seeing anyone at the moment, let alone being in love with anyone else, but he didn't know that. Then it finally happened. Right when I pulled up in front of my garage and placed the gear in park, I burst into tears. I cried *HARD*. I had held in all my anger, frustrations, hurt, confusions, depressions, and sadness and now that I was getting a hint of regret from him, I was feeling even more hurt. I suddenly felt like I was just a weak woman who Sebastian didn't even have a fear of acting up around.

I must have been weak; after all, what other woman would have accepted the ways he had treated me in our marriage, then say, "I'm leaving you for another woman and now I'm done with her I want to come home", knowing I would most likely take him back. He had to know all he had to do was call because I was just 'that woman': forgiving, sympathetic, hopeless romantic blah blah blah. I WAS WEAK!

And I hated that about me. I didn't want to be 'her' anymore. I wanted to be feared, I wanted to be respected, I wanted to be cherished, and I was not. I cried in my car for over twenty minutes. I stopped crying long enough to think about what I'd do next, then I started to cry again because what I thought of next would definitely hurt someone else's relationship. But I didn't care anymore, I just needed him right now. I dialed Victor.

I woke up the next morning feeling well rested; I always seemed to sleep well after a good, hard cry. I recalled the events of the previous night as I lay in bed staring out the window.

I suddenly regretted calling Victor. I was glad he hadn't picked up the phone, but I knew my number was on his caller ID as a missed call, so he'd know I called. I picked up my phone and saw that I have several missed calls and messages from Victor, and one missed call from Sebastian with no voicemail. I had turned the ringer off before I went to sleep, not wanting to be awoken with any calls. I listened to my voice messages. The first message:

"Hey, Oma! It's Victor. I saw that I missed your call a few minutes ago and now I can't reach you. Are you ok? I hope you are. I know we haven't spoken in a while and was pleasantly surprised to see your number, but upset I missed your call. Call me back as soon as you get this. Hope you're well. Talk to you soon."

Humm... I thought to myself, he sounded so good; his voice was so calming and smooth. I listened to his second message: he had called twenty minutes after his first message:

"Hey! It's Victor again. I'm trying not to worry here, but I really do hope you're ok. Call me back. I'm guessing you may have fallen asleep, but if I don't hear from you by tomorrow afternoon, I'm coming over. Call me." He was always protective of me and I liked that he showed concern for me. Then, I saw he had left me a text message early that morning at 6:15 a.m. "Hey! You up?"

I looked at the time and saw it was 6:38 a.m. I pulled up his number and dialed him.

"Hello? Oma?" Victor picked up on the first ring.

"Hey, handsome," I responded back in my still sleepy voice, feeling comfortable enough to 'pet-name' him.

"Hey, yourself, beautiful," he said. I felt happy that he was responsive to me and sounded comfortable, too. "What's going on? I tried calling you back several times last night. Did you fall asleep?"

"Humm umm..." I playfully moaned back. "I had a long and stressful day and thought about you. I really needed my friend."

A brief silence from Victor. "Oma, you know I'm always here for you. I'm sorry I missed your call. I left my phone in the den when I went to make myself something to eat in the kitchen, and by the time I saw your missed call and tried you back, you didn't answer. You must have gone right to bed. You doing ok? What was wrong?"

I suddenly became overwhelmed with emotions again. I hadn't realized how much I had missed him. I missed our friendship especially: our talks, coffee runs, movie nights and such. I let a tear or two fall from my eyes to my ears as I lay on my back in bed, and quickly wiped them away.

"I am now. What are you up to today?" I asked, hoping he and I would meet up to catch up.

"Well, I cleared my schedule for today for the possibility of hearing back from you. If you hadn't called me back, I was planning on coming over to check on you, and if you weren't home, I was gonna go out looking for you till I found you. And I said to myself, if you *did* answer when I was planning on calling you again this morning, that something must have been wrong because it's highly unusual for you to call me at night, so I was gonna hang out with you today anyway to make sure you were ok. So long story short, I'm yours."

Why didn't I date this guy before I got married, again? My heart was suddenly lighter. Even if he was just kidding, it still felt nice to hear.

"I need my friend again. I miss you, Vic."

"I miss you, too, Oma. Listen, I'm gonna be over there in twenty. Put on your sweats; we're going for a walk," he said.

"Okay," I responded with a smile, and then hung up.

I rolled around my bed for a minute or so more, then got up, brushed my teeth, washed my face, washed my pitts and vaginal area with a soapy wash-cloth, put on deodorant and then some lotion; put on my pink and black work-out outfit and matching tennis shoes. I was excited to see Victor again and had a burst of energy from the excitement. When I got downstairs, the nanny was preparing breakfast for the kids who were still asleep.

"Good morning, Ms. Oma! You go out?" Teresa was from Mexico and had been with us since both kids were born and she had become like a mother figure to us all. She lived with us and had become a part of the family.

"Yeah. I'm just going for a walk. Everything ok down here? You need anything from the store?" I asked.

"No. Everything ok, Ms. Oma. No problem."

"Ok, I'll be back soon. Thank you, Teresa."

I went out through the garage door, expecting Victor to arrive at any time. While I was pulling my sunglasses out from my sunglass holder in my car, Victor pulled up in my driveway in his red truck. He got out and we both exchanged a smile as we began walking towards each other. We embraced tightly for a long time and my nerves went calm. Boy, had I missed him.

We sat on a bench after over two hours of walking and talking, catching up on married life, work, projects and everything in-between.

"Oma, I'm so sorry to hear about you and Sebastian. I really am sorry you had to go through that kind of pain. I wish you had called me sooner. You didn't have to go through that alone, Oma. You know I would have been there for you, no matter where we were in our relationship," Victor said as he held my hand.

"I know, Vic, but I didn't want it to come off as a *now that he's gone, I'm gonna move on to you* rebound. You know I can't live like that." I responded.

"I know, Oma, and honestly, that's exactly why I love you. I'll never stop. Ever." He looked at me, then took my face gently in his hand, moved in and kissed me.

"Oma?" He pulled away gently and lifted my now tear-filled face.

"Vic," I whispered. "I love you, too, Vic." He gently wiped my tears away and kissed me again, and I felt love.

Victor and I were obviously in love with each other, and we had now verbalized it to each other. But being in love and being together are two very separate and difficult things. I was still married and I knew Sebastian and I still had a chance because I still loved him, too; plus, I still didn't want a divorce. And Victor was also still married, and I knew he would leave his wife for me, if I left my husband.

Life had just gotten a whole lot more complicated.

About the Author

UZO AMAKA, was born in Oakland California to a Nigerian Father and an American Mother and raised in Nigeria for ten years from ages two to twelve.

In 2003, she graduated from San Francisco State University with a Bachelor degree in Broadcasting and Electronic Communications while also obtaining her Real Estate License that same year. A year later, she obtained her Real Estate Broker's license and established her own company *Epitome Real Estate Investment.* In 2009, Uzo obtained her nursing license and continues to work both as a Real Estate Broker and a Registered Nurse.

Uzo has been married to the same loving man for over eleven years, have 2 beautiful children and live in the Bay Area.

Uzo enjoys taking road trips with her family, traveling, dancing, organizing events for family and writing (Letters, poems, stories etc). *Ages of Suffocation: Remembered Dreams* is Uzo's first book.

To send questions or comments to Uzo Amaka, you may contact her on social media sites:

Facebook: www.facebook.com/uzo07

Twitter: @theonlyuzo

YouTube: Uzo Amaka (theonlyuzo@gmail.com) or

Website: www.theonlyuzo.com

www.ingramcontent.com/pod-product-compliance
Lightning Source LLC
Chambersburg PA
CBHW061142040426
42445CB00013B/1511